55 Chicken Recipes for Home

By: Kelly Johnson

Table of Contents

- Classic Roast Chicken
- Chicken Parmesan
- Grilled Chicken Skewers
- Chicken Stir-Fry
- Chicken Alfredo Pasta
- Honey Mustard Glazed Chicken
- Chicken Tacos
- Lemon Garlic Chicken
- Coconut Curry Chicken
- Teriyaki Chicken
- Baked Lemon Herb Chicken Thighs
- Chicken and Broccoli Casserole
- Mango Salsa Chicken
- Chicken Piccata
- Buffalo Chicken Wraps
- Mediterranean Chicken Skillet
- Crispy Baked Chicken Wings
- Chicken and Spinach Stuffed Shells
- Chicken Kebabs with Tzatziki Sauce
- Cajun Chicken Pasta
- Sesame Ginger Chicken Stir-Fry
- Chicken Fajitas
- Garlic Parmesan Chicken Wings
- Honey Sriracha Grilled Chicken
- Chicken and Rice Soup
- Pesto Stuffed Chicken Breast
- Jamaican Jerk Chicken
- Caprese Chicken
- Lemon Herb Grilled Chicken Salad
- Chicken Enchiladas
- Butter Chicken (Chicken Makhani)
- Greek Lemon Garlic Roast Chicken
- Chicken Tikka Masala
- Thai Basil Chicken (Pad Krapow Gai)
- Chicken and Mushroom Risotto

- Barbecue Chicken Pizza
- Chicken Satay with Peanut Sauce
- Chicken Shawarma
- Coq au Vin
- Honey Garlic Glazed Chicken Drumsticks
- Chicken Pesto Pasta
- Spanish Chicken and Chorizo Stew
- Lemon Dijon Grilled Chicken
- Crispy Orange Chicken
- Chicken Caesar Salad Wraps
- White Chicken Chili
- Chicken and Vegetable Curry
- Chicken Stuffed Bell Peppers
- Honey Balsamic Glazed Chicken Thighs
- Chicken Florentine
- Szechuan Chicken
- Chicken Quesadillas
- Chicken Coconut Curry Soup
- Cajun Chicken and Rice
- Mango Habanero Grilled Chicken

Classic Roast Chicken

Ingredients:

- 1 whole chicken (about 4-5 pounds)
- Salt and black pepper to taste
- 2 tablespoons olive oil or melted butter
- 1 teaspoon dried thyme or rosemary (optional)
- 1 lemon, halved
- 4 cloves garlic, peeled
- 1 onion, quartered
- 2 carrots, chopped
- 2 celery stalks, chopped

Instructions:

Preheat the Oven:
- Preheat your oven to 425°F (220°C).

Prepare the Chicken:
- Remove the giblets from the chicken cavity, if any. Pat the chicken dry with paper towels.
- Season the chicken cavity with salt and pepper.

Season the Exterior:
- Rub the outside of the chicken with olive oil or melted butter. Season generously with salt, pepper, and dried thyme or rosemary, if using.

Stuff the Chicken:
- Place lemon halves, garlic cloves, and a few sprigs of herbs (if available) inside the chicken cavity.

Truss the Chicken (Optional):
- Trussing helps the chicken cook more evenly. You can use kitchen twine to tie the legs together.

Prepare Vegetables:
- In a roasting pan, scatter chopped onions, carrots, and celery. Place the chicken on top.

Roast in the Oven:
- Roast the chicken in the preheated oven for about 1 to 1.5 hours or until the internal temperature reaches 165°F (74°C).

Baste the Chicken:

- Every 30 minutes, baste the chicken with the pan juices. This helps keep it moist and flavorful.

Rest and Carve:
- Once cooked, remove the chicken from the oven and let it rest for about 10-15 minutes before carving.

Serve:
- Carve the chicken and serve with the roasted vegetables and pan juices.

This classic roast chicken is versatile, and you can customize the seasoning to your liking. Enjoy your delicious and comforting roast chicken!

Chicken Parmesan

Ingredients:

For the Chicken:

- 4 boneless, skinless chicken breasts
- Salt and black pepper, to taste
- 1 cup all-purpose flour
- 2 large eggs, beaten
- 2 cups Italian-style breadcrumbs
- 1 cup grated Parmesan cheese
- Olive oil, for frying

For the Assembly:

- 2 cups marinara sauce (homemade or store-bought)
- 1 1/2 cups shredded mozzarella cheese
- 1/2 cup grated Parmesan cheese
- Fresh basil or parsley for garnish (optional)

Instructions:

Preheat the Oven:
- Preheat your oven to 375°F (190°C).

Prepare the Chicken:
- If the chicken breasts are thick, you can slice them horizontally to create thinner cutlets. Season both sides with salt and pepper.

Breading the Chicken:
- Dredge each chicken cutlet in the flour, then dip into the beaten eggs, and coat with a mixture of breadcrumbs and grated Parmesan cheese.

Fry the Chicken:
- Heat olive oil in a large skillet over medium-high heat. Fry the breaded chicken cutlets until golden brown on both sides. Transfer them to a paper towel-lined plate to absorb excess oil.

Assemble in a Baking Dish:
- In a baking dish, spread a thin layer of marinara sauce. Place the fried chicken cutlets on top. Spoon more marinara sauce over each cutlet.

Add Cheese:

- Sprinkle shredded mozzarella and grated Parmesan cheese over each chicken cutlet.

Bake in the Oven:
- Bake in the preheated oven for about 20-25 minutes or until the cheese is melted and bubbly.

Garnish and Serve:
- Remove from the oven and let it rest for a few minutes. Garnish with fresh basil or parsley if desired. Serve over cooked pasta or with a side of your choice.

Enjoy your delicious Chicken Parmesan!

Grilled Chicken Skewers

Ingredients:

For the Marinade:

- 1.5 to 2 pounds boneless, skinless chicken breasts, cut into cubes
- 1/4 cup olive oil
- 3 tablespoons soy sauce
- 2 tablespoons honey
- 2 cloves garlic, minced
- 1 teaspoon ground cumin
- 1 teaspoon paprika
- 1 teaspoon dried oregano
- Salt and black pepper, to taste

For the Skewers:

- Wooden or metal skewers (if using wooden skewers, soak them in water for about 30 minutes to prevent burning)
- Bell peppers, cherry tomatoes, onions, or any other vegetables of your choice, cut into bite-sized pieces

Instructions:

Prepare the Marinade:
- In a bowl, whisk together olive oil, soy sauce, honey, minced garlic, cumin, paprika, dried oregano, salt, and black pepper.

Marinate the Chicken:
- Place the chicken cubes in a large resealable plastic bag or a shallow dish. Pour the marinade over the chicken, ensuring it is well-coated. Marinate in the refrigerator for at least 30 minutes, or ideally 2-4 hours for more flavor.

Assemble the Skewers:
- Preheat your grill or grill pan. Thread the marinated chicken cubes onto the skewers, alternating with the vegetables.

Grill the Skewers:
- Grill the skewers over medium-high heat for about 10-15 minutes, turning occasionally, until the chicken is fully cooked and has a nice char on the edges.

Serve:
- Remove the skewers from the grill and let them rest for a few minutes. Serve the grilled chicken skewers with your favorite dipping sauce, such as tzatziki, barbecue sauce, or a squeeze of lemon.

These grilled chicken skewers are versatile, and you can customize the vegetables and marinade to suit your taste. Enjoy your delicious and simple grilled chicken skewers!

Chicken Stir-Fry

Ingredients:

For the Stir-Fry:

- 1.5 to 2 pounds boneless, skinless chicken breasts or thighs, thinly sliced
- 2 tablespoons soy sauce
- 1 tablespoon oyster sauce
- 1 tablespoon hoisin sauce
- 1 tablespoon cornstarch
- 1 tablespoon vegetable oil
- 1 onion, thinly sliced
- 2 bell peppers (different colors), thinly sliced
- 1 cup broccoli florets
- 2 carrots, julienned
- 3 cloves garlic, minced
- 1 tablespoon ginger, minced
- 1 cup snap peas, ends trimmed
- 2 green onions, sliced (for garnish)

For the Sauce:

- 3 tablespoons soy sauce
- 2 tablespoons oyster sauce
- 1 tablespoon hoisin sauce
- 1 tablespoon rice vinegar
- 1 tablespoon brown sugar

Optional:

- Sesame seeds and sliced green onions for garnish
- Cooked rice or noodles for serving

Instructions:

Prepare the Chicken:

- In a bowl, combine the sliced chicken with soy sauce, oyster sauce, hoisin sauce, and cornstarch. Allow it to marinate for at least 15-30 minutes.

Make the Sauce:
- In a small bowl, whisk together the soy sauce, oyster sauce, hoisin sauce, rice vinegar, and brown sugar. Set aside.

Stir-Fry:
- Heat vegetable oil in a large wok or skillet over medium-high heat. Add the marinated chicken and stir-fry until it's browned and cooked through. Remove the chicken from the wok and set it aside.

Vegetables:
- In the same wok, add a bit more oil if needed. Stir-fry the garlic and ginger until fragrant. Add onions, bell peppers, broccoli, carrots, and snap peas. Stir-fry for 3-5 minutes or until the vegetables are crisp-tender.

Combine and Sauce:
- Return the cooked chicken to the wok with the vegetables. Pour the prepared sauce over the mixture and toss everything together until well coated and heated through.

Serve:
- Serve the chicken stir-fry over cooked rice or noodles. Garnish with sliced green onions and sesame seeds if desired.

Feel free to customize the vegetables and adjust the sauce to your taste. Enjoy your delicious chicken stir-fry!

Chicken Alfredo Pasta

Ingredients:

- 8 oz (225g) fettuccine pasta
- 2 boneless, skinless chicken breasts, cut into bite-sized pieces
- Salt and black pepper to taste
- 2 tablespoons olive oil
- 3 cloves garlic, minced
- 1 cup heavy cream
- 1 cup grated Parmesan cheese
- 1/2 cup unsalted butter
- Salt and black pepper to taste
- Fresh parsley, chopped (for garnish)

Instructions:

Cook the Pasta:
- Cook the fettuccine pasta according to package instructions until al dente. Drain and set aside.

Season and Cook Chicken:
- Season the chicken pieces with salt and pepper. In a large skillet, heat olive oil over medium-high heat. Add the chicken and cook until browned and cooked through. Remove the chicken from the skillet and set aside.

Prepare Alfredo Sauce:
- In the same skillet, add minced garlic and sauté for about 1 minute until fragrant. Add the butter and let it melt. Pour in the heavy cream and bring it to a gentle simmer. Stir in the Parmesan cheese until it melts and the sauce thickens.

Combine Chicken and Pasta:
- Add the cooked chicken pieces back to the skillet, stirring to coat them in the Alfredo sauce. Allow the mixture to simmer for a few minutes until heated through.

Combine with Pasta:
- Add the cooked fettuccine pasta to the skillet, tossing it with the Alfredo sauce and chicken until well coated. Season with additional salt and pepper to taste.

Garnish and Serve:

- Garnish with chopped fresh parsley. Serve immediately, optionally with extra Parmesan cheese on the side.

Enjoy your delicious and creamy Chicken Alfredo Pasta! You can also add vegetables like broccoli or peas for extra flavor and nutrition.

Honey Mustard Glazed Chicken

Ingredients:

For the Marinade:

- 4 boneless, skinless chicken breasts
- 1/4 cup Dijon mustard
- 1/4 cup honey
- 2 tablespoons whole grain mustard
- 2 tablespoons soy sauce
- 2 cloves garlic, minced
- Salt and black pepper to taste

For Garnish:

- Fresh parsley, chopped

Instructions:

Prepare the Marinade:
- In a bowl, whisk together Dijon mustard, honey, whole grain mustard, soy sauce, minced garlic, salt, and black pepper.

Marinate the Chicken:
- Place the chicken breasts in a resealable plastic bag or shallow dish. Pour half of the marinade over the chicken, ensuring it's well-coated. Reserve the other half for later. Marinate in the refrigerator for at least 30 minutes to allow the flavors to meld.

Cook the Chicken:
- Preheat your grill or grill pan over medium-high heat. Remove the chicken from the marinade and discard the used marinade.
- Grill the chicken for about 6-8 minutes per side, or until fully cooked and the internal temperature reaches 165°F (74°C). Baste the chicken with the reserved marinade during the last few minutes of cooking.

Garnish and Serve:
- Once cooked, transfer the chicken to a serving platter. Garnish with chopped fresh parsley for added freshness.

Serve:
- Serve the Honey Mustard Glazed Chicken with your favorite side dishes, such as roasted vegetables, rice, or a fresh salad.

Enjoy your flavorful and succulent Honey Mustard Glazed Chicken!

Chicken Tacos

Ingredients:

For the Chicken:

- 1.5 to 2 pounds boneless, skinless chicken breasts or thighs, thinly sliced
- 2 tablespoons olive oil
- 1 tablespoon chili powder
- 1 teaspoon cumin
- 1 teaspoon paprika
- 1 teaspoon garlic powder
- Salt and black pepper to taste
- Juice of 1 lime

For Serving:

- Small taco-sized flour or corn tortillas
- Shredded lettuce
- Diced tomatoes
- Shredded cheese (cheddar, Monterey Jack, or Mexican blend)
- Salsa or pico de gallo
- Sour cream
- Fresh cilantro, chopped
- Lime wedges

Instructions:

Prepare the Chicken:
- In a bowl, combine olive oil, chili powder, cumin, paprika, garlic powder, salt, pepper, and lime juice. Add the sliced chicken and toss to coat evenly. Let it marinate for at least 15-30 minutes.

Cook the Chicken:
- Heat a large skillet over medium-high heat. Add the marinated chicken and cook until fully cooked and slightly charred, about 5-7 minutes per side.

Warm the Tortillas:

- In a dry skillet or on a griddle, warm the tortillas for about 20 seconds on each side or until they are pliable.

Assemble the Tacos:
- Place a spoonful of the cooked chicken onto each tortilla. Top with shredded lettuce, diced tomatoes, shredded cheese, salsa, sour cream, and chopped cilantro.

Serve:
- Serve the chicken tacos immediately with lime wedges on the side for squeezing.

Feel free to customize your chicken tacos with your favorite toppings and sauces. You can also add guacamole, sliced avocado, or pickled onions for extra flavor. Enjoy your delicious homemade chicken tacos!

Lemon Garlic Chicken

Ingredients:

- 4 boneless, skinless chicken breasts
- Salt and black pepper to taste
- 2 tablespoons olive oil
- 4 cloves garlic, minced
- Zest of 1 lemon
- Juice of 2 lemons
- 1 teaspoon dried thyme or rosemary (optional)
- 1/2 cup chicken broth or white wine
- Fresh parsley, chopped (for garnish)

Instructions:

Prepare the Chicken:
- Season the chicken breasts with salt and black pepper on both sides.

Sear the Chicken:
- In a large skillet, heat olive oil over medium-high heat. Add the chicken breasts and sear them for 4-5 minutes on each side or until golden brown and cooked through. Remove the chicken from the skillet and set aside.

Saute Garlic and Lemon Zest:
- In the same skillet, add minced garlic and lemon zest. Sauté for about 1-2 minutes until the garlic becomes fragrant.

Deglaze with Broth/Wine:
- Pour in the chicken broth or white wine, scraping the bottom of the skillet to release any flavorful bits. Allow it to simmer for a couple of minutes.

Add Lemon Juice:
- Squeeze the juice of two lemons into the skillet, stirring to combine.

Return Chicken to Skillet:
- Return the seared chicken to the skillet. If using, sprinkle dried thyme or rosemary over the chicken.

Simmer:
- Allow the chicken to simmer in the lemon-garlic sauce for an additional 5-7 minutes, ensuring the chicken is cooked through and has absorbed the flavors.

Garnish and Serve:

- Garnish with chopped fresh parsley and serve the Lemon Garlic Chicken with your favorite side dishes, such as rice, quinoa, or roasted vegetables.

Enjoy your succulent and citrusy Lemon Garlic Chicken!

Coconut Curry Chicken

Ingredients:

- 1.5 to 2 pounds boneless, skinless chicken thighs or breasts, cut into bite-sized pieces
- Salt and black pepper to taste
- 2 tablespoons vegetable oil or coconut oil
- 1 large onion, finely chopped
- 3 cloves garlic, minced
- 1 tablespoon ginger, minced
- 2 tablespoons red curry paste
- 1 tablespoon yellow curry powder
- 1 can (14 oz) coconut milk
- 1 cup chicken broth
- 1 tablespoon soy sauce
- 1 tablespoon fish sauce (optional)
- 1 tablespoon brown sugar
- Vegetables of your choice (bell peppers, carrots, broccoli, etc.)
- Fresh cilantro, chopped (for garnish)
- Cooked rice for serving

Instructions:

Season and Sear Chicken:
- Season chicken pieces with salt and black pepper. In a large skillet or wok, heat the oil over medium-high heat. Add the chicken and brown it on all sides. Once browned, remove the chicken from the skillet and set aside.

Saute Aromatics:
- In the same skillet, add more oil if needed. Add chopped onions, minced garlic, and minced ginger. Sauté until the onions are soft and fragrant.

Add Curry Paste and Powder:
- Stir in the red curry paste and curry powder, cooking for 1-2 minutes until the spices are aromatic.

Incorporate Coconut Milk:
- Pour in the coconut milk, chicken broth, soy sauce, and fish sauce (if using). Stir well to combine, bringing the mixture to a simmer.

Simmer Chicken:

- Return the seared chicken to the skillet. Cover and let it simmer for about 15-20 minutes, or until the chicken is cooked through.

Add Vegetables:
- Add your choice of vegetables to the curry. Simmer until the vegetables are tender-crisp, usually for an additional 5-7 minutes.

Adjust Seasoning:
- Taste the curry and adjust the seasoning with additional salt, soy sauce, or brown sugar if needed.

Serve:
- Serve the Coconut Curry Chicken over cooked rice. Garnish with chopped cilantro.

Enjoy your delicious and aromatic Coconut Curry Chicken!

Teriyaki Chicken

Ingredients:

- 1.5 to 2 pounds boneless, skinless chicken thighs or breasts, cut into bite-sized pieces
- Salt and black pepper to taste
- 1 tablespoon vegetable oil
- 1/2 cup soy sauce
- 1/4 cup mirin (sweet rice wine)
- 2 tablespoons sake or dry white wine
- 2 tablespoons brown sugar
- 1 tablespoon honey
- 2 cloves garlic, minced
- 1 tablespoon ginger, grated
- 1 tablespoon cornstarch (optional, for thickening)
- Sesame seeds and sliced green onions for garnish
- Cooked rice for serving

Instructions:

Season and Sear Chicken:
- Season chicken pieces with salt and black pepper. In a large skillet or wok, heat the vegetable oil over medium-high heat. Add the chicken and brown it on all sides.

Prepare Teriyaki Sauce:
- In a bowl, whisk together soy sauce, mirin, sake or white wine, brown sugar, honey, minced garlic, and grated ginger.

Cook Chicken:
- Pour the teriyaki sauce over the browned chicken in the skillet. Bring it to a simmer and let it cook for about 15-20 minutes, or until the chicken is cooked through, and the sauce thickens slightly.

Thicken Sauce (Optional):
- If you prefer a thicker sauce, mix cornstarch with a little water to create a slurry. Stir it into the teriyaki sauce and cook for an additional 2-3 minutes until the sauce thickens.

Garnish and Serve:
- Garnish the Teriyaki Chicken with sesame seeds and sliced green onions. Serve over cooked rice.

Enjoy your homemade Teriyaki Chicken! You can also add steamed vegetables like broccoli or snow peas for extra flavor and texture.

Baked Lemon Herb Chicken Thighs

Ingredients:

- 4-6 bone-in, skin-on chicken thighs
- Salt and black pepper to taste
- 2 tablespoons olive oil
- 3 cloves garlic, minced
- Zest of 1 lemon
- Juice of 1 lemon
- 1 teaspoon dried thyme
- 1 teaspoon dried rosemary
- 1 teaspoon dried oregano
- 1 teaspoon paprika
- Fresh herbs (such as parsley or thyme) for garnish

Instructions:

Preheat the Oven:
- Preheat your oven to 400°F (200°C).

Prepare the Chicken Thighs:
- Pat the chicken thighs dry with paper towels. Season both sides with salt and black pepper.

Create Herb Mixture:
- In a small bowl, mix together olive oil, minced garlic, lemon zest, lemon juice, dried thyme, dried rosemary, dried oregano, and paprika.

Coat Chicken Thighs:
- Place the chicken thighs in a baking dish. Brush each thigh with the herb and lemon mixture, ensuring they are well-coated.

Bake in the Oven:
- Bake in the preheated oven for about 30-40 minutes or until the chicken reaches an internal temperature of 165°F (74°C) and the skin is crispy and golden.

Baste (Optional):
- Optionally, baste the chicken with the juices from the pan halfway through the cooking time for extra flavor.

Garnish and Serve:
- Once cooked, remove the chicken from the oven. Garnish with fresh herbs and serve hot.

Serve with Side Dishes:
- Serve the Baked Lemon Herb Chicken Thighs with your favorite side dishes, such as roasted vegetables, mashed potatoes, or a fresh salad.

Enjoy your flavorful and juicy Baked Lemon Herb Chicken Thighs!

Chicken and Broccoli Casserole

Ingredients:

- 2 cups cooked chicken, shredded or diced
- 3 cups broccoli florets, blanched or steamed
- 2 cups cooked white rice
- 1 1/2 cups shredded cheddar cheese
- 1/2 cup mayonnaise
- 1/2 cup sour cream
- 1/2 cup chicken broth
- 2 cloves garlic, minced
- 1 teaspoon onion powder
- Salt and black pepper to taste
- 1 cup breadcrumbs (for topping)
- 2 tablespoons melted butter (for topping)

Instructions:

Preheat the Oven:
- Preheat your oven to 350°F (175°C).

Prepare the Casserole Dish:
- Grease a baking dish or casserole dish with cooking spray or butter.

Combine Chicken, Broccoli, and Rice:
- In a large mixing bowl, combine cooked chicken, broccoli florets, cooked white rice, and shredded cheddar cheese.

Make the Sauce:
- In a separate bowl, whisk together mayonnaise, sour cream, chicken broth, minced garlic, onion powder, salt, and black pepper.

Combine Sauce with Chicken Mixture:
- Pour the sauce over the chicken mixture and gently toss until everything is well coated.

Transfer to Baking Dish:
- Transfer the mixture to the prepared baking dish, spreading it out evenly.

Prepare the Topping:
- In a small bowl, combine breadcrumbs with melted butter. Sprinkle this mixture over the top of the casserole.

Bake in the Oven:

- Bake in the preheated oven for 25-30 minutes or until the casserole is hot and bubbly, and the top is golden brown.

Serve:
- Remove from the oven and let it rest for a few minutes before serving. Serve the Chicken and Broccoli Casserole hot.

This casserole is a complete meal on its own, but you can also serve it with a side salad or additional vegetables. Enjoy your comforting Chicken and Broccoli Casserole!

Mango Salsa Chicken

Ingredients:

- 4 boneless, skinless chicken breasts
- Salt and black pepper to taste
- 1 tablespoon olive oil

For Mango Salsa:

- 2 ripe mangos, peeled, pitted, and diced
- 1/2 red onion, finely chopped
- 1 red bell pepper, diced
- 1 jalapeño, seeds removed and finely chopped (optional for heat)
- 1/4 cup fresh cilantro, chopped
- Juice of 2 limes
- Salt to taste

Instructions:

Prepare Mango Salsa:
- In a bowl, combine diced mangos, red onion, red bell pepper, jalapeño (if using), cilantro, lime juice, and salt. Toss the ingredients together and set aside to let the flavors meld.

Prepare Chicken:
- Preheat your grill or oven to medium-high heat. Season chicken breasts with salt and black pepper. Drizzle with olive oil to coat.

Grill or Bake Chicken:
- Grill the chicken for about 6-8 minutes per side, or until fully cooked, with beautiful grill marks. Alternatively, you can bake the chicken in a preheated oven at 400°F (200°C) for approximately 20-25 minutes, or until the internal temperature reaches 165°F (74°C).

Rest and Serve:
- Let the grilled or baked chicken rest for a few minutes before serving.

Top with Mango Salsa:
- Spoon the mango salsa generously over each chicken breast.

Garnish and Serve:

- Garnish with additional cilantro if desired. Serve the Mango Salsa Chicken with your favorite side dishes, such as rice, quinoa, or a fresh salad.

Enjoy the delightful combination of juicy mango salsa and perfectly cooked chicken!

This dish is perfect for a light and flavorful meal.

Chicken Piccata

Ingredients:

- 4 boneless, skinless chicken breasts
- Salt and black pepper to taste
- 1 cup all-purpose flour, for dredging
- 4 tablespoons unsalted butter
- 4 tablespoons olive oil
- 1/3 cup fresh lemon juice (about 2 lemons)
- 1/2 cup chicken broth
- 1/4 cup brined capers, rinsed
- 1/4 cup fresh parsley, chopped (for garnish)
- Lemon slices, for garnish
- Cooked pasta or rice, for serving (optional)

Instructions:

Prepare the Chicken:
- Pat the chicken breasts dry with paper towels. Season both sides with salt and black pepper.

Dredge in Flour:
- Dredge the chicken in the flour, shaking off any excess.

Cook the Chicken:
- In a large skillet, heat 2 tablespoons of butter and 2 tablespoons of olive oil over medium-high heat. Add the chicken breasts and cook for about 3-4 minutes per side, or until golden brown and cooked through. Remove the chicken from the skillet and set aside.

Make the Sauce:
- In the same skillet, add the remaining butter, olive oil, lemon juice, chicken broth, and capers. Scrape any browned bits from the bottom of the skillet. Bring the sauce to a simmer and let it cook for 2-3 minutes to reduce slightly.

Return Chicken to the Skillet:
- Return the cooked chicken to the skillet, spooning the sauce over each piece. Simmer for an additional 2-3 minutes to heat through.

Garnish and Serve:
- Garnish the Chicken Piccata with chopped parsley and lemon slices.

Serve with Pasta or Rice (Optional):
- Optionally, serve the Chicken Piccata over cooked pasta or rice, allowing the sauce to coat the pasta.

Enjoy your Chicken Piccata with its zesty lemon-caper sauce! It pairs well with a side of vegetables or a simple green salad.

Buffalo Chicken Wraps

Ingredients:

- 2 cups cooked and shredded chicken (rotisserie or cooked at home)
- 1/2 cup buffalo sauce (adjust to taste)
- 2 tablespoons unsalted butter, melted
- 4 large tortillas or wraps
- 1 cup shredded lettuce
- 1 cup diced tomatoes
- 1/2 cup diced red onion
- 1/2 cup crumbled blue cheese or ranch dressing
- Ranch or blue cheese dressing for drizzling (optional)
- Fresh cilantro or parsley for garnish (optional)

Instructions:

Prepare Buffalo Chicken:
- In a bowl, mix the shredded chicken with buffalo sauce and melted butter until well coated.

Assemble Wraps:
- Lay out the tortillas. Divide the shredded lettuce, diced tomatoes, red onion, and buffalo chicken equally among the wraps.

Add Blue Cheese or Dressing:
- Sprinkle crumbled blue cheese over the chicken mixture or drizzle with ranch dressing if you prefer a milder flavor.

Roll the Wraps:
- Fold in the sides of each tortilla and then roll them up tightly from the bottom to create a wrap.

Serve:
- Place the wraps seam-side down on a serving platter. Optionally, drizzle with additional ranch or blue cheese dressing and garnish with fresh cilantro or parsley.

Slice and Enjoy:
- Slice the wraps in half diagonally and serve immediately.

These Buffalo Chicken Wraps are great for a quick lunch or dinner. Feel free to customize them by adding avocado, cucumber, or other favorite toppings. Enjoy the bold and zesty flavors!

Mediterranean Chicken Skillet

Ingredients:

- 4 boneless, skinless chicken breasts
- Salt and black pepper to taste
- 2 tablespoons olive oil
- 4 cloves garlic, minced
- 1 teaspoon dried oregano
- 1 teaspoon dried thyme
- 1 teaspoon dried rosemary
- 1 cup cherry tomatoes, halved
- 1/2 cup Kalamata olives, pitted and halved
- 1/2 cup artichoke hearts, drained and chopped
- 1/2 cup crumbled feta cheese
- Juice of 1 lemon
- Fresh parsley, chopped, for garnish

Instructions:

Prepare the Chicken:
- Season the chicken breasts with salt and black pepper on both sides.

Cook Chicken in Skillet:
- In a large skillet, heat olive oil over medium-high heat. Add the chicken breasts and sear for about 4-5 minutes per side or until golden brown and cooked through. Remove the chicken from the skillet and set aside.

Saute Aromatics:
- In the same skillet, add minced garlic, dried oregano, dried thyme, and dried rosemary. Sauté for about 1-2 minutes until fragrant.

Combine Ingredients:
- Add halved cherry tomatoes, halved Kalamata olives, and chopped artichoke hearts to the skillet. Stir to combine.

Return Chicken to Skillet:
- Return the cooked chicken to the skillet, nestling it into the vegetable mixture.

Add Feta Cheese and Lemon Juice:
- Sprinkle crumbled feta cheese over the chicken and vegetables. Squeeze the juice of one lemon over the entire skillet.

Finish Cooking:

- Cover the skillet and let it simmer for an additional 5-7 minutes, allowing the flavors to meld and the feta to soften.

Garnish and Serve:
- Garnish with chopped fresh parsley and serve the Mediterranean Chicken Skillet hot.

This dish is delicious on its own or can be served with couscous, quinoa, or crusty bread to soak up the flavorful juices. Enjoy your Mediterranean-inspired meal!

Crispy Baked Chicken Wings

Ingredients:

For the Chicken Wings:

- 2 pounds chicken wings, split at joints, tips discarded
- 1 tablespoon baking powder (not baking soda)
- 1 teaspoon salt
- 1 teaspoon black pepper
- 1 teaspoon garlic powder
- 1 teaspoon onion powder
- 1/2 teaspoon smoked paprika (optional for extra flavor)

For the Sauce (Optional):

- 1/2 cup hot sauce (like Frank's RedHot)
- 1/4 cup unsalted butter, melted
- 1 tablespoon honey or maple syrup (optional for sweetness)
- 1 teaspoon garlic powder
- Salt to taste

Instructions:

Preheat the Oven:
- Preheat your oven to 425°F (220°C).

Dry and Season Chicken Wings:
- Pat the chicken wings dry with paper towels. In a bowl, mix baking powder, salt, black pepper, garlic powder, onion powder, and smoked paprika. Toss the wings in this mixture until evenly coated.

Arrange on Baking Sheet:
- Place a wire rack on a baking sheet. Arrange the seasoned wings on the rack, ensuring they are not touching each other. This allows air to circulate and helps them become crispy.

Bake:
- Bake the wings in the preheated oven for about 45-50 minutes, or until golden brown and crispy. Flip the wings halfway through the cooking time to ensure even crispiness.

Make Sauce (Optional):

- While the wings are baking, prepare the sauce by mixing hot sauce, melted butter, honey or maple syrup (if using), garlic powder, and salt in a bowl. Adjust the heat and sweetness according to your preference.

Toss Wings in Sauce (Optional):
- Once the wings are done baking, transfer them to a large bowl. Pour the sauce over the wings and toss until they are evenly coated.

Serve:
- Serve the Crispy Baked Chicken Wings immediately. You can garnish with chopped fresh parsley or celery sticks and blue cheese or ranch dressing on the side.

Enjoy your crispy and flavorful baked chicken wings!

Chicken and Spinach Stuffed Shells

Ingredients:

- 1 box (12 oz) jumbo pasta shells
- 2 cups cooked chicken, shredded (rotisserie chicken works well)
- 2 cups fresh spinach, chopped
- 2 cups ricotta cheese
- 1 cup mozzarella cheese, shredded
- 1/2 cup Parmesan cheese, grated
- 1 egg
- 2 cloves garlic, minced
- 1 teaspoon dried oregano
- 1 teaspoon dried basil
- Salt and black pepper to taste
- 1 jar (24 oz) marinara sauce
- Fresh basil or parsley for garnish (optional)

Instructions:

Preheat the Oven:
- Preheat your oven to 350°F (175°C).

Cook Pasta Shells:
- Cook the jumbo pasta shells according to the package instructions. Drain and set aside.

Prepare Filling:
- In a large bowl, combine shredded chicken, chopped spinach, ricotta cheese, mozzarella cheese, Parmesan cheese, egg, minced garlic, dried oregano, dried basil, salt, and black pepper. Mix well until all ingredients are evenly combined.

Stuff the Shells:
- Using a spoon, fill each cooked pasta shell with the chicken and spinach mixture.

Assemble in Baking Dish:
- Spread a thin layer of marinara sauce in the bottom of a baking dish. Arrange the stuffed shells in the dish.

Top with Marinara Sauce:
- Pour the remaining marinara sauce over the stuffed shells, ensuring they are well-covered.

Bake in the Oven:
- Cover the baking dish with foil and bake in the preheated oven for about 25-30 minutes or until the shells are heated through.

Garnish and Serve:
- Remove from the oven and garnish with fresh basil or parsley if desired. Serve the Chicken and Spinach Stuffed Shells hot.

These stuffed shells make for a satisfying meal on their own, or you can serve them with a side salad or garlic bread. Enjoy your delicious and cheesy Chicken and Spinach Stuffed Shells!

Chicken Kebabs with Tzatziki Sauce

Ingredients:

For Chicken Kebabs:

- 1.5 to 2 pounds boneless, skinless chicken breasts or thighs, cut into bite-sized pieces
- 2 tablespoons olive oil
- 2 cloves garlic, minced
- 1 teaspoon dried oregano
- 1 teaspoon dried thyme
- 1 teaspoon paprika
- Salt and black pepper to taste
- Wooden or metal skewers

For Tzatziki Sauce:

- 1 cup Greek yogurt
- 1 cucumber, peeled, seeded, and finely diced
- 2 cloves garlic, minced
- 1 tablespoon fresh dill, chopped
- 1 tablespoon fresh mint, chopped
- 1 tablespoon olive oil
- 1 tablespoon lemon juice
- Salt and black pepper to taste

Instructions:

Marinate the Chicken:
- In a bowl, combine the chicken pieces with olive oil, minced garlic, dried oregano, dried thyme, paprika, salt, and black pepper. Allow it to marinate for at least 30 minutes, or preferably longer in the refrigerator.

Prepare Skewers:
- If using wooden skewers, soak them in water for about 30 minutes to prevent burning. Thread the marinated chicken pieces onto the skewers.

Grill or Cook Chicken:

- Preheat your grill or grill pan over medium-high heat. Grill the chicken skewers for about 5-7 minutes per side or until the chicken is cooked through and has a nice char.

Make Tzatziki Sauce:
- In a bowl, combine Greek yogurt, finely diced cucumber, minced garlic, chopped dill, chopped mint, olive oil, lemon juice, salt, and black pepper. Mix well.

Serve:
- Serve the grilled chicken kebabs hot with a side of tzatziki sauce for dipping.

Garnish (Optional):
- Optionally, garnish with additional fresh herbs and a drizzle of olive oil.

Enjoy your delicious Chicken Kebabs with Tzatziki Sauce! These are perfect for a summer barbecue or a delightful dinner.

Cajun Chicken Pasta

Ingredients:

- 8 oz (225g) fettuccine or your choice of pasta
- 2 boneless, skinless chicken breasts, thinly sliced
- 2 tablespoons Cajun seasoning
- Salt and black pepper to taste
- 2 tablespoons olive oil
- 1 red bell pepper, thinly sliced
- 1 yellow bell pepper, thinly sliced
- 1 small red onion, thinly sliced
- 3 cloves garlic, minced
- 1 cup cherry tomatoes, halved
- 1 cup heavy cream
- 1/2 cup chicken broth
- 1/2 cup grated Parmesan cheese
- Fresh parsley, chopped (for garnish)

Instructions:

Cook the Pasta:
- Cook the pasta according to the package instructions until al dente. Drain and set aside.

Season and Cook Chicken:
- Season the thinly sliced chicken breasts with Cajun seasoning, salt, and black pepper. In a large skillet, heat olive oil over medium-high heat. Add the seasoned chicken and cook until browned and cooked through. Remove the chicken from the skillet and set aside.

Saute Vegetables:
- In the same skillet, add sliced red and yellow bell peppers, and red onion. Sauté until the vegetables are tender.

Add Garlic and Tomatoes:
- Add minced garlic and halved cherry tomatoes to the skillet. Cook for an additional 2 minutes until the garlic is fragrant.

Prepare the Sauce:
- Pour in the heavy cream and chicken broth, stirring to combine. Bring the mixture to a simmer.

Add Cheese and Chicken:

- Stir in the grated Parmesan cheese until the sauce thickens. Add the cooked chicken back to the skillet, letting it heat through.

Combine with Pasta:
- Add the cooked pasta to the skillet, tossing it with the Cajun chicken and vegetable mixture until well coated in the creamy sauce.

Garnish and Serve:
- Garnish with chopped fresh parsley. Serve the Cajun Chicken Pasta hot.

Enjoy your spicy and creamy Cajun Chicken Pasta! Adjust the level of Cajun seasoning to your preferred spice level.

Sesame Ginger Chicken Stir-Fry

Ingredients:

For the Stir-Fry:

- 1.5 to 2 pounds boneless, skinless chicken breasts or thighs, thinly sliced
- 2 tablespoons soy sauce
- 1 tablespoon sesame oil
- 1 tablespoon cornstarch
- 2 tablespoons vegetable oil (for cooking)
- 1 bell pepper, thinly sliced
- 1 cup snap peas, ends trimmed
- 1 carrot, julienned
- 3 green onions, sliced
- Sesame seeds for garnish (optional)
- Cooked rice or noodles for serving

For the Sauce:

- 3 tablespoons soy sauce
- 2 tablespoons hoisin sauce
- 1 tablespoon rice vinegar
- 1 tablespoon honey
- 1 tablespoon fresh ginger, minced
- 2 cloves garlic, minced

Instructions:

Marinate the Chicken:
- In a bowl, combine the thinly sliced chicken with 2 tablespoons of soy sauce, 1 tablespoon of sesame oil, and 1 tablespoon of cornstarch. Let it marinate for at least 15-30 minutes.

Prepare the Sauce:
- In a small bowl, whisk together 3 tablespoons of soy sauce, hoisin sauce, rice vinegar, honey, minced ginger, and minced garlic. Set aside.

Cook the Chicken:

- Heat 2 tablespoons of vegetable oil in a large wok or skillet over medium-high heat. Add the marinated chicken and cook until browned and cooked through. Remove the chicken from the wok and set aside.

Stir-Fry Vegetables:
- In the same wok, add a bit more oil if needed. Stir-fry the bell pepper, snap peas, carrot, and green onions until they are crisp-tender.

Combine Chicken and Vegetables:
- Return the cooked chicken to the wok, tossing it with the vegetables.

Add Sauce:
- Pour the prepared sauce over the chicken and vegetables. Toss everything together until well-coated and heated through.

Serve:
- Serve the Sesame Ginger Chicken Stir-Fry over cooked rice or noodles. Garnish with sesame seeds if desired.

Enjoy your quick and flavorful Sesame Ginger Chicken Stir-Fry! Adjust the vegetables to your liking and feel free to add more sesame seeds or sliced green onions for extra freshness.

Chicken Fajitas

Ingredients:

- 1.5 to 2 pounds boneless, skinless chicken breasts or thighs, thinly sliced
- 2 bell peppers (any color), thinly sliced
- 1 large onion, thinly sliced
- 3 tablespoons olive oil
- 2 tablespoons fajita seasoning (store-bought or homemade)
- Juice of 1 lime
- Salt and black pepper to taste
- Flour tortillas for serving
- Toppings: Salsa, sour cream, guacamole, shredded cheese, chopped cilantro, lime wedges, etc.

Instructions:

Marinate the Chicken:
- In a bowl, combine the thinly sliced chicken with fajita seasoning, olive oil, lime juice, salt, and black pepper. Let it marinate for at least 15-30 minutes.

Prepare Vegetables:
- In a separate bowl, toss the sliced bell peppers and onions with a bit of olive oil, salt, and pepper.

Heat the Grill or Skillet:
- Preheat your grill or a large skillet over medium-high heat.

Cook the Chicken:
- Cook the marinated chicken on the grill or in the skillet until browned and cooked through, about 5-7 minutes per side.

Sauté Vegetables:
- In the same skillet or on a griddle, add the sliced bell peppers and onions. Sauté until they are tender-crisp and slightly charred.

Combine Chicken and Vegetables:
- Combine the cooked chicken with the sautéed vegetables, tossing everything together.

Warm Tortillas:
- In a dry skillet or on the grill, warm the flour tortillas for about 20 seconds on each side.

Serve:
- Spoon the chicken and vegetable mixture onto the warmed tortillas. Serve with your favorite toppings such as salsa, sour cream, guacamole, shredded cheese, chopped cilantro, and lime wedges.

Enjoy your delicious and customizable Chicken Fajitas! It's a perfect meal for a casual dinner or entertaining guests.

Garlic Parmesan Chicken Wings

Ingredients:

For Chicken Wings:

- 2 pounds chicken wings, split at joints, tips discarded
- 2 tablespoons olive oil
- Salt and black pepper to taste

For Garlic Parmesan Sauce:

- 1/2 cup unsalted butter
- 4 cloves garlic, minced
- 1/2 cup grated Parmesan cheese
- 1 teaspoon dried oregano
- 1 teaspoon dried parsley
- Salt and black pepper to taste
- Fresh parsley, chopped (for garnish)

Instructions:

Preheat the Oven:
- Preheat your oven to 400°F (200°C).

Prepare Chicken Wings:
- In a large bowl, toss the chicken wings with olive oil, salt, and black pepper until evenly coated.

Bake the Wings:
- Arrange the seasoned chicken wings on a baking sheet lined with parchment paper. Bake in the preheated oven for 45-50 minutes or until the wings are golden brown and crispy, turning them halfway through.

Prepare Garlic Parmesan Sauce:
- In a saucepan over medium heat, melt the butter. Add minced garlic and sauté for about 1-2 minutes until fragrant.

Add Parmesan and Herbs:
- Stir in grated Parmesan cheese, dried oregano, and dried parsley. Continue to stir until the cheese is melted and the sauce is well combined.

Season the Sauce:
- Season the sauce with salt and black pepper to taste. Adjust the seasoning as needed.

Toss Wings in Sauce:
- Once the chicken wings are done baking, transfer them to a large bowl. Pour the garlic Parmesan sauce over the wings and toss until evenly coated.

Garnish and Serve:
- Garnish with chopped fresh parsley and serve the Garlic Parmesan Chicken Wings hot.

Enjoy your crispy and flavorful Garlic Parmesan Chicken Wings! They make for a delicious appetizer or a crowd-pleasing snack.

Honey Sriracha Grilled Chicken

Ingredients:

- 4 boneless, skinless chicken breasts
- Salt and black pepper to taste
- 1/4 cup honey
- 2 tablespoons soy sauce
- 2 tablespoons Sriracha sauce (adjust to taste for spice)
- 2 tablespoons olive oil
- 2 cloves garlic, minced
- 1 tablespoon fresh ginger, grated
- Sesame seeds and chopped green onions for garnish (optional)

Instructions:

Prepare the Marinade:
- In a bowl, whisk together honey, soy sauce, Sriracha sauce, olive oil, minced garlic, and grated ginger. Adjust Sriracha according to your desired level of spiciness.

Marinate the Chicken:
- Place the chicken breasts in a resealable plastic bag or a shallow dish. Pour half of the marinade over the chicken, reserving the other half for later. Seal the bag or cover the dish and let it marinate in the refrigerator for at least 30 minutes to 2 hours.

Preheat the Grill:
- Preheat your grill to medium-high heat.

Grill the Chicken:
- Remove the chicken from the marinade and discard the used marinade. Season the chicken with salt and black pepper. Grill the chicken breasts for about 6-8 minutes per side or until fully cooked and grill marks appear.

Brush with Reserved Marinade:
- During the last few minutes of grilling, brush the chicken with the reserved marinade, turning occasionally to glaze both sides.

Garnish and Serve:
- Once the chicken is fully cooked and has a nice glaze, remove it from the grill. Garnish with sesame seeds and chopped green onions if desired.

Rest and Serve:

- Let the Honey Sriracha Grilled Chicken rest for a few minutes before serving.

Serve the grilled chicken with your favorite side dishes or on top of a fresh salad for a delicious and spicy meal. Enjoy!

Chicken and Rice Soup

Ingredients:

- 1 tablespoon olive oil
- 1 onion, finely chopped
- 2 carrots, peeled and diced
- 2 celery stalks, diced
- 3 cloves garlic, minced
- 1 teaspoon dried thyme
- 1 teaspoon dried rosemary
- 1 bay leaf
- Salt and black pepper to taste
- 1 cup white rice, uncooked
- 8 cups chicken broth (homemade or store-bought)
- 2 cups cooked chicken, shredded or diced
- 1 cup frozen peas
- Fresh parsley, chopped (for garnish)
- Lemon wedges (optional, for serving)

Instructions:

Sauté Aromatics:
- In a large pot or Dutch oven, heat olive oil over medium heat. Add chopped onion, diced carrots, and diced celery. Sauté until the vegetables are softened, about 5 minutes.

Add Garlic and Herbs:
- Add minced garlic, dried thyme, dried rosemary, bay leaf, salt, and black pepper. Cook for an additional 1-2 minutes until the garlic is fragrant.

Add Rice and Broth:
- Stir in the uncooked rice, then pour in the chicken broth. Bring the mixture to a simmer.

Cook Rice:
- Cook the rice according to the package instructions or until it's tender.

Add Cooked Chicken and Peas:
- Add the cooked and shredded (or diced) chicken to the pot, along with frozen peas. Simmer for an additional 5-10 minutes until the peas are cooked through.

Adjust Seasoning:

- Taste the soup and adjust the seasoning if needed. Remove the bay leaf.

Garnish and Serve:
- Ladle the Chicken and Rice Soup into bowls. Garnish with chopped fresh parsley and serve with lemon wedges if desired.

This comforting soup is not only delicious but also easy to make. Feel free to customize it by adding other vegetables or herbs according to your preferences. Enjoy your homemade Chicken and Rice Soup!

Pesto Stuffed Chicken Breast

Ingredients:

For Pesto:

- 2 cups fresh basil leaves, packed
- 1/2 cup grated Parmesan cheese
- 1/2 cup pine nuts or walnuts
- 3 garlic cloves, peeled
- 1/2 cup extra-virgin olive oil
- Salt and black pepper to taste

For Chicken:

- 4 boneless, skinless chicken breasts
- Salt and black pepper to taste
- 1 tablespoon olive oil
- 1 cup mozzarella cheese, shredded
- Cherry tomatoes, for garnish (optional)
- Fresh basil leaves, for garnish (optional)

Instructions:

Prepare Pesto:
- In a food processor, combine fresh basil, grated Parmesan cheese, pine nuts or walnuts, and garlic cloves. Pulse until coarsely chopped.
- With the food processor running, gradually add the olive oil until the pesto reaches your desired consistency. Season with salt and black pepper to taste. Set aside.

Preheat Oven:
- Preheat your oven to 375°F (190°C).

Prepare Chicken Breasts:
- Using a sharp knife, make a horizontal slit along the side of each chicken breast to create a pocket without cutting through the other side.

Season Chicken:

- Season the inside and outside of each chicken breast with salt and black pepper.

Stuff with Pesto:
- Spoon a generous amount of pesto into the pocket of each chicken breast. Sprinkle shredded mozzarella over the pesto.

Secure with Toothpicks:
- Secure the openings with toothpicks to keep the pesto and cheese inside.

Sear Chicken:
- In an oven-safe skillet, heat olive oil over medium-high heat. Sear the chicken breasts on each side for 2-3 minutes until golden brown.

Finish in the Oven:
- Transfer the skillet to the preheated oven and bake for 20-25 minutes or until the chicken is cooked through and the cheese is melted and bubbly.

Garnish and Serve:
- Garnish with cherry tomatoes and fresh basil leaves if desired. Remove toothpicks before serving.

Enjoy your Pesto Stuffed Chicken Breast with a side of vegetables or a light salad for a delicious and satisfying meal!

Jamaican Jerk Chicken

Ingredients:

For Jerk Marinade:

- 4 green onions, chopped
- 3 tablespoons fresh thyme leaves
- 2 tablespoons allspice berries (ground allspice)
- 1 tablespoon black peppercorns
- 1 tablespoon brown sugar
- 1 tablespoon salt
- 1 tablespoon garlic powder
- 1 tablespoon onion powder
- 1 teaspoon ground cinnamon
- 1 teaspoon ground nutmeg
- 1-2 Scotch bonnet peppers, seeds removed (adjust to taste for spice)
- 1/4 cup soy sauce
- 1/4 cup olive oil
- Juice of 2 limes
- 4-6 pounds chicken pieces (drumsticks, thighs, or a whole chicken)

Instructions:

Prepare Jerk Marinade:
- In a food processor or blender, combine green onions, thyme leaves, allspice berries, black peppercorns, brown sugar, salt, garlic powder, onion powder, ground cinnamon, ground nutmeg, Scotch bonnet peppers, soy sauce, olive oil, and lime juice. Blend until you get a smooth paste.

Marinate the Chicken:
- Place the chicken pieces in a large bowl or a zip-top bag. Coat the chicken with the jerk marinade, ensuring each piece is well covered. Marinate in the refrigerator for at least 2 hours, preferably overnight for more flavor.

Preheat the Grill or Oven:
- Preheat your grill or oven to medium-high heat.

Grill or Bake Chicken:
- If grilling, cook the marinated chicken on the preheated grill, turning occasionally, until the chicken is cooked through and has a nice char,

about 30-45 minutes. If baking, preheat the oven to 375°F (190°C) and bake the chicken in a roasting pan for approximately 45-60 minutes or until fully cooked.

Rest and Serve:
- Let the Jamaican Jerk Chicken rest for a few minutes before serving.

Serve the Jamaican Jerk Chicken with your favorite side dishes, such as rice and peas, plantains, or a fresh tropical fruit salad. Enjoy the bold and spicy flavors!

Caprese Chicken

Ingredients:

- 4 boneless, skinless chicken breasts
- Salt and black pepper to taste
- 2 tablespoons olive oil
- 4 cloves garlic, minced
- 1 cup cherry tomatoes, halved
- 1/2 cup fresh mozzarella balls or pearls
- Fresh basil leaves, torn or chopped
- Balsamic glaze or balsamic reduction, for drizzling

Instructions:

Season and Cook Chicken:
- Season the chicken breasts with salt and black pepper. In a large skillet, heat olive oil over medium-high heat. Add the chicken breasts and cook for about 5-7 minutes per side or until fully cooked and golden brown. Remove the chicken from the skillet and set aside.

Sauté Garlic and Tomatoes:
- In the same skillet, add minced garlic and sauté for about 1-2 minutes until fragrant. Add the halved cherry tomatoes and cook for an additional 2-3 minutes until the tomatoes are slightly softened.

Assemble Caprese Chicken:
- Return the cooked chicken to the skillet, nestling it among the sautéed tomatoes. Add fresh mozzarella balls or pearls to the skillet.

Garnish with Basil:
- Sprinkle torn or chopped fresh basil leaves over the chicken and tomatoes.

Drizzle with Balsamic Glaze:
- Drizzle balsamic glaze or balsamic reduction over the Caprese Chicken.

Serve:
- Serve the Caprese Chicken hot, making sure to spoon some of the tomatoes, mozzarella, and basil over each chicken breast.

This dish pairs well with a side of pasta, rice, or a simple green salad. The combination of fresh tomatoes, creamy mozzarella, and aromatic basil creates a light and satisfying meal. Enjoy your Caprese Chicken!

Lemon Herb Grilled Chicken Salad

Ingredients:

For Lemon Herb Grilled Chicken:

- 4 boneless, skinless chicken breasts
- Salt and black pepper to taste
- Zest and juice of 2 lemons
- 3 tablespoons olive oil
- 2 cloves garlic, minced
- 1 teaspoon dried oregano
- 1 teaspoon dried thyme
- 1 teaspoon dried rosemary

For Salad:

- Mixed salad greens (lettuce, spinach, arugula, etc.)
- Cherry tomatoes, halved
- Cucumber, sliced
- Red onion, thinly sliced
- Feta cheese, crumbled
- Kalamata olives, pitted
- Lemon wedges (for serving)

For Lemon Herb Vinaigrette:

- 1/4 cup extra-virgin olive oil
- Zest and juice of 1 lemon
- 1 tablespoon Dijon mustard
- 1 tablespoon honey or maple syrup
- Salt and black pepper to taste

Instructions:

    Prepare Lemon Herb Marinade:

- In a bowl, whisk together lemon zest, lemon juice, olive oil, minced garlic, dried oregano, dried thyme, dried rosemary, salt, and black pepper.

Marinate Chicken:
- Place the chicken breasts in a shallow dish or a zip-top bag. Pour the lemon herb marinade over the chicken, ensuring each piece is well coated. Marinate in the refrigerator for at least 30 minutes to 2 hours.

Preheat the Grill:
- Preheat your grill to medium-high heat.

Grill Chicken:
- Remove the chicken from the marinade and grill for about 6-8 minutes per side or until fully cooked and has a nice char. Let the chicken rest for a few minutes before slicing.

Prepare Salad Greens:
- In a large salad bowl, toss the mixed greens, cherry tomatoes, cucumber slices, red onion slices, crumbled feta cheese, and Kalamata olives.

Make Lemon Herb Vinaigrette:
- In a small bowl, whisk together extra-virgin olive oil, lemon zest, lemon juice, Dijon mustard, honey or maple syrup, salt, and black pepper.

Assemble Salad:
- Slice the grilled chicken and arrange it on top of the salad. Drizzle the Lemon Herb Vinaigrette over the salad.

Serve:
- Serve the Lemon Herb Grilled Chicken Salad with additional lemon wedges on the side.

This salad is perfect for a light and flavorful meal. The combination of grilled chicken and the zesty lemon herb dressing creates a delightful and satisfying dish. Enjoy!

Chicken Enchiladas

Ingredients:

For the Enchilada Filling:

- 2 cups cooked and shredded chicken (rotisserie chicken works well)
- 1 cup black beans, drained and rinsed
- 1 cup corn kernels (fresh, frozen, or canned)
- 1 cup shredded Mexican blend cheese
- 1/2 cup diced red onion
- 1 teaspoon ground cumin
- 1 teaspoon chili powder
- Salt and black pepper to taste
- 1/4 cup fresh cilantro, chopped

For the Enchilada Sauce:

- 2 tablespoons olive oil
- 2 tablespoons all-purpose flour
- 2 tablespoons chili powder
- 1 teaspoon ground cumin
- 1/2 teaspoon garlic powder
- 1/2 teaspoon onion powder
- 1/4 teaspoon dried oregano
- 1/4 teaspoon cayenne pepper (optional, for heat)
- 2 cups chicken broth
- 1 can (8 oz) tomato sauce
- Salt to taste

For Assembly:

- 10-12 small flour tortillas
- 1 cup shredded cheese (for topping)
- Fresh cilantro, chopped (for garnish)
- Sour cream and sliced green onions for serving (optional)

Instructions:

Preheat the Oven:

- Preheat your oven to 375°F (190°C).

Prepare Enchilada Filling:
- In a large bowl, combine shredded chicken, black beans, corn, shredded cheese, diced red onion, ground cumin, chili powder, salt, black pepper, and chopped cilantro. Mix well.

Prepare Enchilada Sauce:
- In a saucepan, heat olive oil over medium heat. Add flour, chili powder, ground cumin, garlic powder, onion powder, dried oregano, and cayenne pepper. Cook for 1-2 minutes, stirring constantly.
- Gradually whisk in chicken broth and tomato sauce. Bring to a simmer and cook until the sauce thickens, about 5-7 minutes. Season with salt to taste.

Assemble Enchiladas:
- Spread a small amount of enchilada sauce in the bottom of a baking dish.
- Place a portion of the chicken filling onto each tortilla, roll them up, and place them seam-side down in the baking dish.

Pour Sauce and Add Cheese:
- Pour the remaining enchilada sauce over the rolled tortillas. Sprinkle shredded cheese over the top.

Bake:
- Bake in the preheated oven for 20-25 minutes or until the cheese is melted and bubbly.

Garnish and Serve:
- Garnish with chopped cilantro. Serve the Chicken Enchiladas hot with optional toppings like sour cream and sliced green onions.

Enjoy your delicious and comforting Chicken Enchiladas!

Butter Chicken (Chicken Makhani)

Ingredients:

For Marinating Chicken:

- 1.5 pounds (about 700g) boneless, skinless chicken thighs or breasts, cut into bite-sized pieces
- 1 cup plain yogurt
- 1 tablespoon ginger-garlic paste
- 1 teaspoon turmeric powder
- 1 teaspoon chili powder
- 1 teaspoon ground cumin
- 1 teaspoon ground coriander
- Salt to taste

For Butter Chicken Sauce:

- 3 tablespoons unsalted butter
- 1 large onion, finely chopped
- 3 cloves garlic, minced
- 1 tablespoon ginger, minced
- 1 teaspoon ground turmeric
- 1 teaspoon ground cumin
- 1 teaspoon ground coriander
- 1 teaspoon garam masala
- 1 teaspoon chili powder (adjust to taste)
- 1 can (15 oz) tomato sauce or puree
- 1 cup heavy cream
- 1 tablespoon honey or sugar (adjust to taste)
- Salt to taste
- Fresh cilantro, chopped (for garnish)
- Cooked basmati rice or naan (for serving)

Instructions:

Marinate Chicken:
- In a bowl, combine chicken pieces with yogurt, ginger-garlic paste, turmeric powder, chili powder, ground cumin, ground coriander, and salt.

- Allow it to marinate for at least 30 minutes to an hour, preferably longer in the refrigerator.

Cook Marinated Chicken:
- Preheat the oven to 400°F (200°C). Place the marinated chicken on a baking sheet and bake for about 20-25 minutes or until the chicken is cooked through.

Prepare Butter Chicken Sauce:
- In a large skillet or pan, melt butter over medium heat. Add finely chopped onion and sauté until golden brown.

Add Aromatics:
- Add minced garlic and ginger to the skillet. Sauté for 1-2 minutes until fragrant.

Spices and Tomato Sauce:
- Stir in ground turmeric, ground cumin, ground coriander, garam masala, and chili powder. Cook for another 1-2 minutes.
- Add tomato sauce or puree to the skillet, stirring well to combine. Cook for 5-7 minutes, allowing the sauce to thicken.

Blend the Sauce:
- If desired, use an immersion blender or transfer the sauce to a blender to achieve a smooth consistency.

Finish Butter Chicken:
- Return the cooked chicken to the skillet. Stir in heavy cream and honey or sugar. Allow it to simmer for 10-15 minutes, allowing the flavors to meld.

Adjust Seasoning:
- Season with salt to taste. Adjust the sweetness and spice levels if needed.

Garnish and Serve:
- Garnish with chopped cilantro. Serve the Butter Chicken over cooked basmati rice or with naan.

Enjoy your homemade Butter Chicken with its creamy and flavorful sauce!

Greek Lemon Garlic Roast Chicken

Ingredients:

- 1 whole chicken (about 4-5 pounds)
- Salt and black pepper to taste
- 1 tablespoon dried oregano
- 1 tablespoon dried thyme
- 1 tablespoon dried rosemary
- 4 cloves garlic, minced
- Zest of 1 lemon
- Juice of 2 lemons
- 1/4 cup olive oil
- 1/2 cup chicken broth or white wine (optional)
- Fresh oregano and lemon slices for garnish

Instructions:

Preheat the Oven:
- Preheat your oven to 375°F (190°C).

Prepare the Chicken:
- Pat the chicken dry with paper towels. Season the chicken inside and out with salt and black pepper.

Make Herb-Garlic Mixture:
- In a small bowl, mix together dried oregano, dried thyme, dried rosemary, minced garlic, lemon zest, lemon juice, and olive oil to create an herb-garlic mixture.

Rub the Chicken:
- Rub the herb-garlic mixture all over the chicken, ensuring it's evenly coated. You can also gently lift the skin and rub some of the mixture directly onto the meat.

Truss the Chicken (Optional):
- Truss the chicken by tying the legs together with kitchen twine. This helps the chicken cook more evenly.

Roast the Chicken:
- Place the seasoned and trussed chicken in a roasting pan or on a baking sheet. Roast in the preheated oven for about 1 hour and 15 minutes, or until the internal temperature reaches 165°F (74°C). Baste the chicken with pan juices every 20-30 minutes.

Add Broth or Wine (Optional):
- If using, you can add chicken broth or white wine to the pan about halfway through the cooking time to enhance flavors and keep the chicken moist.

Rest and Garnish:
- Once the chicken is done, remove it from the oven and let it rest for 10-15 minutes before carving. Garnish with fresh oregano and lemon slices.

Serve:
- Serve the Greek Lemon Garlic Roast Chicken with your favorite sides, such as roasted vegetables, potatoes, or a Greek salad.

Enjoy the aromatic and succulent Greek Lemon Garlic Roast Chicken with its vibrant Mediterranean flavors!

Chicken Tikka Masala

Ingredients:

For Chicken Marinade:

- 1.5 pounds (about 700g) boneless, skinless chicken thighs or breasts, cut into bite-sized pieces
- 1 cup plain yogurt
- 1 tablespoon ginger-garlic paste
- 1 teaspoon ground turmeric
- 1 teaspoon ground cumin
- 1 teaspoon chili powder
- 1 teaspoon garam masala
- 1 teaspoon smoked paprika
- Salt to taste
- Juice of 1 lemon

For Tikka Masala Sauce:

- 2 tablespoons vegetable oil or ghee
- 1 large onion, finely chopped
- 3 cloves garlic, minced
- 1 tablespoon ginger, minced
- 1 teaspoon ground coriander
- 1 teaspoon ground cumin
- 1 teaspoon chili powder
- 1 teaspoon turmeric powder
- 1 teaspoon garam masala
- 1 teaspoon paprika
- 1 can (15 oz) tomato sauce or puree
- 1 cup heavy cream
- Salt to taste
- Fresh cilantro, chopped (for garnish)
- Cooked basmati rice or naan (for serving)

Instructions:

Marinate Chicken:

- In a bowl, combine chicken pieces with yogurt, ginger-garlic paste, ground turmeric, ground cumin, chili powder, garam masala, smoked paprika, salt, and lemon juice. Allow it to marinate for at least 30 minutes to an hour, preferably longer in the refrigerator.

Grill or Bake Chicken:
- Preheat the grill or oven to medium-high heat. Thread the marinated chicken pieces onto skewers and grill or bake for about 15-20 minutes or until fully cooked and slightly charred.

Prepare Tikka Masala Sauce:
- In a large skillet or pan, heat vegetable oil or ghee over medium heat. Add finely chopped onion and sauté until golden brown.

Add Aromatics and Spices:
- Add minced garlic and ginger to the skillet. Sauté for 1-2 minutes until fragrant. Stir in ground coriander, ground cumin, chili powder, turmeric powder, garam masala, and paprika. Cook for another 1-2 minutes.

Add Tomato Sauce:
- Pour in tomato sauce or puree, stirring well to combine. Simmer for 5-7 minutes, allowing the sauce to thicken.

Finish Tikka Masala:
- Reduce the heat to low. Stir in heavy cream and cooked chicken pieces. Simmer for an additional 10-15 minutes, allowing the flavors to meld. Season with salt to taste.

Garnish and Serve:
- Garnish with chopped cilantro. Serve Chicken Tikka Masala over cooked basmati rice or with naan.

Enjoy your homemade Chicken Tikka Masala with its creamy and aromatic sauce!

Thai Basil Chicken (Pad Krapow Gai)

Ingredients:

- 1 lb ground chicken
- 2 tablespoons vegetable oil
- 4 cloves garlic, minced
- 2 Thai bird chilies, finely chopped (adjust to taste)
- 1 bell pepper, thinly sliced
- 1 onion, thinly sliced
- 1 cup fresh basil leaves, preferably Thai basil
- Salt and black pepper to taste

For the Sauce:

- 3 tablespoons oyster sauce
- 1 tablespoon soy sauce
- 1 tablespoon fish sauce
- 1 teaspoon sugar

Instructions:

Prepare the Sauce:
- In a small bowl, whisk together oyster sauce, soy sauce, fish sauce, and sugar. Set aside.

Cook Ground Chicken:
- In a wok or a large skillet, heat vegetable oil over medium-high heat. Add minced garlic and chopped Thai bird chilies. Stir-fry for about 30 seconds until fragrant.

Add Ground Chicken:
- Add the ground chicken to the wok. Break it up with a spatula and cook until it's browned and cooked through.

Add Vegetables:
- Add sliced bell pepper and onion to the wok. Stir-fry for a few minutes until the vegetables are slightly softened but still crisp.

Add Sauce and Basil:
- Pour the prepared sauce over the chicken and vegetables. Stir well to coat everything in the sauce. Add fresh basil leaves and toss until the basil is wilted.

Season and Adjust:
- Season with salt and black pepper to taste. Adjust the sauce or spice level if needed.

Serve:
- Serve the Thai Basil Chicken over steamed jasmine rice. Optionally, you can top it with a fried egg for extra richness.

Enjoy your homemade Thai Basil Chicken, a delicious and quick Thai stir-fry with bold flavors

Chicken and Mushroom Risotto

Ingredients:

- 1.5 cups Arborio rice
- 1 lb boneless, skinless chicken breasts, cut into bite-sized pieces
- 8 oz mushrooms, sliced (cremini or button mushrooms work well)
- 1 onion, finely chopped
- 2 cloves garlic, minced
- 4 cups chicken broth, kept warm
- 1 cup dry white wine (optional)
- 1/2 cup grated Parmesan cheese
- 2 tablespoons butter
- 2 tablespoons olive oil
- Salt and black pepper to taste
- Fresh parsley, chopped (for garnish)

Instructions:

Prepare Chicken:
- Season the chicken pieces with salt and black pepper. In a large skillet or pan, heat 1 tablespoon of olive oil over medium-high heat. Add the chicken and cook until browned and cooked through. Remove from the pan and set aside.

Sauté Mushrooms:
- In the same pan, add another tablespoon of olive oil. Sauté the sliced mushrooms until they release their moisture and become golden brown. Remove some mushrooms for garnish if desired. Set aside.

Cook Onions and Garlic:
- In the same pan, add the chopped onion and cook until softened. Add minced garlic and cook for an additional 1-2 minutes until fragrant.

Add Arborio Rice:
- Add Arborio rice to the pan and stir to coat it with the oil, onions, and garlic. Toast the rice for 1-2 minutes until it becomes translucent around the edges.

Deglaze with Wine (Optional):
- If using wine, pour it into the pan and stir until it's mostly absorbed by the rice.

Add Warm Chicken Broth:

- Begin adding the warm chicken broth one ladle at a time, stirring frequently. Allow the liquid to be mostly absorbed before adding the next ladle. Continue this process until the rice is creamy and cooked to al dente texture.

Add Chicken and Mushrooms:
- Stir in the cooked chicken and sautéed mushrooms.

Finish with Butter and Cheese:
- Remove the risotto from heat. Stir in butter and grated Parmesan cheese until creamy and smooth.

Season and Garnish:
- Season the risotto with salt and black pepper to taste. Garnish with chopped fresh parsley and the reserved sautéed mushrooms.

Serve Immediately:
- Serve the Chicken and Mushroom Risotto hot, with additional Parmesan cheese if desired.

Enjoy your creamy and flavorful Chicken and Mushroom Risotto!

Barbecue Chicken Pizza

Ingredients:

For the Pizza:

- 1 pizza dough (store-bought or homemade)
- 1 cup cooked and shredded chicken (rotisserie chicken works well)
- 1/2 cup barbecue sauce (plus extra for drizzling)
- 1 cup shredded mozzarella cheese
- 1/2 red onion, thinly sliced
- 1/2 cup sliced bell peppers (any color)
- 1/4 cup fresh cilantro, chopped
- Cornmeal or flour (for dusting)

For Garnish:

- Ranch dressing or blue cheese dressing (optional)
- Red pepper flakes (optional)

Instructions:

Preheat the Oven:
- Preheat your oven according to the pizza dough package instructions or to 475°F (245°C).

Prepare Pizza Dough:
- If using store-bought pizza dough, follow the package instructions for bringing it to room temperature. If using homemade dough, roll it out on a floured surface into your desired pizza shape.

Assemble Pizza:
- Place the rolled-out pizza dough on a pizza stone, baking sheet, or pizza pan that's been lightly dusted with cornmeal or flour.
- Spread a layer of barbecue sauce over the pizza dough, leaving a small border around the edges.
- Evenly distribute the shredded chicken over the barbecue sauce.
- Sprinkle shredded mozzarella cheese over the chicken.
- Scatter thinly sliced red onions and bell peppers on top.

Bake the Pizza:
- Place the pizza in the preheated oven and bake according to the dough instructions or until the crust is golden and the cheese is melted and bubbly.

Finish and Garnish:
- Once out of the oven, drizzle additional barbecue sauce over the top for extra flavor.
- Garnish the barbecue chicken pizza with chopped cilantro.
- Optionally, drizzle with ranch dressing or blue cheese dressing and sprinkle red pepper flakes for added kick.

Slice and Serve:
- Allow the pizza to cool for a few minutes, then slice it into wedges and serve.

Enjoy your homemade Barbecue Chicken Pizza, a perfect combination of smoky, savory, and cheesy flavors!

Chicken Satay with Peanut Sauce

Ingredients:

For Chicken Satay:

- 1.5 lbs boneless, skinless chicken thighs, cut into thin strips
- 1/4 cup soy sauce
- 2 tablespoons fish sauce
- 2 tablespoons brown sugar
- 2 tablespoons vegetable oil
- 1 tablespoon curry powder
- 1 teaspoon turmeric powder
- 2 cloves garlic, minced
- Wooden skewers, soaked in water for at least 30 minutes

For Peanut Sauce:

- 1/2 cup creamy peanut butter
- 1/4 cup soy sauce
- 2 tablespoons brown sugar
- 1 tablespoon rice vinegar
- 1 teaspoon sesame oil
- 1 teaspoon grated ginger
- 1 clove garlic, minced
- 1/4 cup water (adjust for desired consistency)
- Lime wedges and chopped cilantro for garnish

Instructions:

Marinate Chicken:
- In a bowl, whisk together soy sauce, fish sauce, brown sugar, vegetable oil, curry powder, turmeric powder, and minced garlic. Add the chicken strips to the marinade, ensuring they are well-coated. Marinate for at least 30 minutes, or preferably, refrigerate for a few hours or overnight.

Thread Chicken onto Skewers:
- Preheat the grill or grill pan. Thread the marinated chicken strips onto the soaked wooden skewers.

Grill Chicken Satay:

- Grill the chicken skewers for about 4-5 minutes per side or until fully cooked and charred. Make sure to turn them occasionally for even cooking.

Prepare Peanut Sauce:
- While the chicken is grilling, prepare the peanut sauce. In a saucepan over low heat, combine peanut butter, soy sauce, brown sugar, rice vinegar, sesame oil, grated ginger, minced garlic, and water. Stir until smooth and well combined. Adjust the consistency with more water if needed.

Garnish and Serve:
- Once the chicken skewers are done, garnish with chopped cilantro and lime wedges.
- Serve the Chicken Satay with Peanut Sauce on the side for dipping.

Enjoy your Chicken Satay with Peanut Sauce as an appetizer or main dish. It's a perfect balance of savory, sweet, and nutty flavors!

Chicken Shawarma

Ingredients:

For Marinating Chicken:

- 1.5 lbs boneless, skinless chicken thighs or breasts, thinly sliced
- 1/4 cup plain yogurt
- 3 tablespoons olive oil
- 4 cloves garlic, minced
- 1 teaspoon ground cumin
- 1 teaspoon ground coriander
- 1 teaspoon ground paprika
- 1 teaspoon ground turmeric
- 1 teaspoon ground cinnamon
- 1 teaspoon ground cayenne pepper (adjust to taste)
- Salt and black pepper to taste

For Tahini Sauce:

- 1/2 cup tahini
- 2 tablespoons lemon juice
- 2 tablespoons water
- 1 clove garlic, minced
- Salt to taste

For Serving:

- Flatbreads or pita bread
- Sliced tomatoes
- Sliced cucumbers
- Red onion slices
- Fresh parsley, chopped

Instructions:

Marinate Chicken:
- In a bowl, mix together yogurt, olive oil, minced garlic, ground cumin, ground coriander, ground paprika, ground turmeric, ground cinnamon, cayenne pepper, salt, and black pepper. Add the sliced chicken, ensuring

it's well coated in the marinade. Cover and refrigerate for at least 1-2 hours or overnight.

Preheat the Grill or Skillet:
- Preheat your grill or a skillet over medium-high heat.

Grill Chicken:
- Thread the marinated chicken slices onto skewers or cook them directly on the grill. Grill for about 5-7 minutes per side or until the chicken is fully cooked and has a nice char.

Prepare Tahini Sauce:
- While the chicken is grilling, prepare the tahini sauce. In a bowl, whisk together tahini, lemon juice, water, minced garlic, and salt. Adjust the consistency with more water if needed.

Assemble Chicken Shawarma:
- Warm the flatbreads or pita bread. Spread a generous amount of tahini sauce on each bread.
- Place grilled chicken slices on top of the sauce.
- Add sliced tomatoes, cucumbers, red onion, and chopped parsley.

Roll and Serve:
- Roll the bread around the filling, creating a wrap or sandwich.

Serve:
- Serve Chicken Shawarma wraps immediately, and enjoy!

Feel free to customize your Chicken Shawarma with your favorite toppings and serve with additional sides like hummus or a Mediterranean salad.

Coq au Vin

Ingredients:

- 1 whole chicken, cut into serving pieces (or use chicken thighs and drumsticks)
- Salt and black pepper to taste
- 4 tablespoons all-purpose flour, for dredging
- 4 tablespoons unsalted butter
- 4 slices bacon, diced
- 1 onion, finely chopped
- 2 carrots, peeled and sliced
- 2 cloves garlic, minced
- 1 bottle (750 ml) red wine (such as Burgundy or Pinot Noir)
- 2 cups chicken broth
- 2 tablespoons tomato paste
- 1 bouquet garni (a bundle of herbs like thyme, parsley, and a bay leaf tied together)
- 1 pound mushrooms, quartered
- Fresh parsley, chopped (for garnish)

Instructions:

Prepare Chicken:
- Season the chicken pieces with salt and black pepper. Dredge the chicken in flour, shaking off excess.

Brown Chicken:
- In a large, heavy pot or Dutch oven, heat 2 tablespoons of butter over medium-high heat. Brown the chicken pieces on all sides. Work in batches if necessary to avoid overcrowding the pot. Remove the chicken and set aside.

Cook Bacon and Aromatics:
- In the same pot, add the diced bacon and cook until crispy. Add the chopped onion, sliced carrots, and minced garlic. Sauté until the vegetables are softened.

Deglaze with Wine:
- Pour in the red wine, scraping the bottom of the pot to release any browned bits. Bring the mixture to a simmer.

Add Chicken Back In:

- Return the browned chicken to the pot. Add chicken broth, tomato paste, and the bouquet garni. Bring it to a simmer, then reduce the heat to low. Cover and let it simmer for about 1.5 to 2 hours, or until the chicken is tender and cooked through.

Sauté Mushrooms:
- In a separate pan, melt the remaining 2 tablespoons of butter. Add the quartered mushrooms and sauté until they are browned and tender.

Finish and Serve:
- Add the sautéed mushrooms to the pot with the chicken and simmer for an additional 15-20 minutes to meld the flavors. Adjust seasoning if needed.

Garnish and Serve:
- Discard the bouquet garni. Garnish with chopped fresh parsley and serve Coq au Vin hot over mashed potatoes, pasta, or crusty bread.

Coq au Vin is a hearty and flavorful dish, perfect for a special occasion or a cozy family dinner. Enjoy!

Chicken Pesto Pasta

Ingredients:

- 8 oz (about 225g) pasta (penne, fusilli, or your choice)
- 1 lb (about 450g) boneless, skinless chicken breasts, cut into bite-sized pieces
- Salt and black pepper to taste
- 2 tablespoons olive oil
- 3/4 cup basil pesto sauce (store-bought or homemade)
- 1 cup cherry tomatoes, halved
- 1/2 cup grated Parmesan cheese
- Fresh basil leaves, for garnish (optional)
- Pine nuts, toasted (optional)

Instructions:

Cook Pasta:
- Cook the pasta according to package instructions in a large pot of salted boiling water until al dente. Drain and set aside.

Season and Cook Chicken:
- Season the chicken pieces with salt and black pepper. In a large skillet, heat olive oil over medium-high heat. Add the chicken and cook until browned and cooked through, about 5-7 minutes.

Combine Chicken with Pesto:
- Reduce the heat to low, add the cooked pasta to the skillet with the chicken. Pour the basil pesto sauce over the chicken and pasta. Toss everything together until well coated.

Add Cherry Tomatoes:
- Add the halved cherry tomatoes to the skillet and gently toss until they are evenly distributed.

Serve:
- Sprinkle grated Parmesan cheese over the pasta and toss once more to combine. If desired, garnish with fresh basil leaves and toasted pine nuts.

Adjust Seasoning and Serve:
- Taste and adjust the seasoning with salt and black pepper if needed. Serve the Chicken Pesto Pasta immediately.

Enjoy your Chicken Pesto Pasta, a simple and flavorful dish that's perfect for a quick and delicious meal!

Spanish Chicken and Chorizo Stew

Ingredients:

- 1.5 lbs (about 700g) chicken thighs, bone-in, skin-on
- Salt and black pepper to taste
- 2 tablespoons olive oil
- 8 oz (about 225g) Spanish chorizo, sliced
- 1 onion, finely chopped
- 3 cloves garlic, minced
- 1 red bell pepper, chopped
- 1 yellow bell pepper, chopped
- 1 can (14 oz) diced tomatoes
- 1 teaspoon smoked paprika
- 1 teaspoon ground cumin
- 1 teaspoon dried oregano
- 1 bay leaf
- 1 cup chicken broth
- 1 can (15 oz) chickpeas, drained and rinsed
- Fresh parsley, chopped (for garnish)

Instructions:

Season and Brown Chicken:
- Season the chicken thighs with salt and black pepper. In a large, oven-safe pot or Dutch oven, heat olive oil over medium-high heat. Brown the chicken thighs on both sides. Remove them from the pot and set aside.

Sauté Chorizo and Aromatics:
- Add sliced chorizo to the pot and sauté until it releases its oils. Add chopped onion and garlic, and sauté until softened.

Add Vegetables:
- Stir in chopped red and yellow bell peppers. Cook for a few minutes until they start to soften.

Combine Tomatoes and Spices:
- Add diced tomatoes, smoked paprika, ground cumin, dried oregano, and bay leaf to the pot. Stir to combine.

Return Chicken to the Pot:

- Return the browned chicken thighs to the pot, nestling them into the vegetable mixture.

Pour in Broth:
- Pour in chicken broth to the pot, ensuring the chicken is partially submerged. Bring the mixture to a simmer.

Bake:
- Preheat your oven to 375°F (190°C). Cover the pot and transfer it to the preheated oven. Bake for about 30-40 minutes, or until the chicken is cooked through and tender.

Add Chickpeas:
- Stir in drained and rinsed chickpeas, allowing them to warm through.

Garnish and Serve:
- Garnish the stew with chopped fresh parsley before serving. Adjust seasoning with salt and pepper if needed.

Serve the Spanish Chicken and Chorizo Stew with crusty bread, rice, or potatoes for a complete and satisfying meal. Enjoy the rich and savory flavors!

Lemon Dijon Grilled Chicken

Ingredients:

- 4 boneless, skinless chicken breasts
- 1/4 cup Dijon mustard
- 1/4 cup olive oil
- Zest of 1 lemon
- Juice of 1 lemon
- 2 cloves garlic, minced
- 1 tablespoon honey
- 1 teaspoon dried thyme
- Salt and black pepper to taste
- Fresh parsley, chopped (for garnish)

Instructions:

Prepare Marinade:
- In a bowl, whisk together Dijon mustard, olive oil, lemon zest, lemon juice, minced garlic, honey, dried thyme, salt, and black pepper.

Marinate Chicken:
- Place the chicken breasts in a resealable plastic bag or shallow dish. Pour half of the marinade over the chicken, ensuring it's well-coated. Reserve the other half for basting and serving. Seal the bag or cover the dish and refrigerate for at least 30 minutes to marinate. For more flavor, you can marinate for a few hours or overnight.

Preheat Grill:
- Preheat your grill to medium-high heat.

Grill Chicken:
- Remove the chicken from the marinade and discard the used marinade. Place the chicken on the preheated grill and cook for about 6-8 minutes per side, or until the internal temperature reaches 165°F (74°C) and the chicken is cooked through. Baste the chicken with the reserved marinade during grilling.

Rest and Garnish:
- Remove the chicken from the grill and let it rest for a few minutes before serving. Garnish with chopped fresh parsley.

Serve:

- Serve the Lemon Dijon Grilled Chicken hot, drizzled with any remaining marinade.

This dish pairs well with a variety of sides, such as roasted vegetables, rice, or a fresh salad. Enjoy the vibrant and citrusy flavors of this grilled chicken!

Crispy Orange Chicken

Ingredients:

For the Chicken:

- 1.5 lbs boneless, skinless chicken thighs, cut into bite-sized pieces
- 1 cup cornstarch
- 1/2 cup all-purpose flour
- 1 teaspoon baking powder
- Salt and black pepper to taste
- 1 cup buttermilk
- Vegetable oil for frying

For the Orange Sauce:

- 1 cup orange juice (freshly squeezed or store-bought)
- 1/2 cup chicken broth
- 1/4 cup soy sauce
- 1/4 cup rice vinegar
- 1/3 cup granulated sugar
- 2 tablespoons cornstarch
- 1 tablespoon orange zest
- 2 cloves garlic, minced
- 1 teaspoon grated ginger
- 2 tablespoons vegetable oil
- Green onions, chopped (for garnish)
- Sesame seeds (optional, for garnish)

Instructions:

Prepare the Chicken:
- In a bowl, mix together cornstarch, all-purpose flour, baking powder, salt, and black pepper.
- Dip the chicken pieces in buttermilk, then coat them in the flour mixture, shaking off any excess.

Fry the Chicken:

- Heat vegetable oil in a deep fryer or large, deep skillet to 350°F (175°C). Fry the coated chicken pieces in batches until golden brown and crispy. Remove and place on a paper towel-lined plate to drain excess oil.

Prepare Orange Sauce:
- In a separate saucepan, heat 2 tablespoons of vegetable oil over medium heat. Add minced garlic and grated ginger, and sauté for about 1 minute until fragrant.
- In a bowl, whisk together orange juice, chicken broth, soy sauce, rice vinegar, granulated sugar, cornstarch, and orange zest until well combined. Pour the mixture into the saucepan with the garlic and ginger.

Cook Orange Sauce:
- Cook the sauce over medium heat, stirring constantly, until it thickens and becomes glossy. This should take about 5-7 minutes.

Combine Sauce and Chicken:
- Once the sauce is ready, add the fried chicken pieces to the sauce. Toss until the chicken is well-coated in the orange sauce.

Garnish and Serve:
- Garnish the Crispy Orange Chicken with chopped green onions and sesame seeds if desired. Serve over steamed rice or with your favorite side.

Enjoy the sweet, tangy, and crispy goodness of homemade Crispy Orange Chicken!

Chicken Caesar Salad Wraps

Ingredients:

For Grilled Chicken:

- 1 lb boneless, skinless chicken breasts
- Salt and black pepper to taste
- 1 tablespoon olive oil
- 1 teaspoon garlic powder
- 1 teaspoon dried oregano
- 1 teaspoon dried thyme

For Caesar Dressing:

- 1/2 cup mayonnaise
- 1/4 cup grated Parmesan cheese
- 2 tablespoons lemon juice
- 1 tablespoon Dijon mustard
- 2 teaspoons Worcestershire sauce
- 1 clove garlic, minced
- Salt and black pepper to taste

For Salad Wraps:

- Large tortillas or wraps
- Romaine lettuce, chopped
- Croutons
- Grated Parmesan cheese
- Cherry tomatoes, halved

Instructions:

Grill Chicken:
- Season the chicken breasts with salt, black pepper, garlic powder, dried oregano, and dried thyme. Heat olive oil in a grill pan or skillet over medium-high heat. Grill the chicken for about 6-8 minutes per side or until fully cooked. Let it rest for a few minutes before slicing.

Prepare Caesar Dressing:

- In a bowl, whisk together mayonnaise, grated Parmesan cheese, lemon juice, Dijon mustard, Worcestershire sauce, minced garlic, salt, and black pepper. Adjust the seasoning to your taste.

Slice Chicken:
- Slice the grilled chicken into thin strips.

Assemble Wraps:
- Lay out the tortillas or wraps. Spread a generous amount of Caesar dressing over each tortilla.
- Place chopped Romaine lettuce on top of the dressing.
- Arrange sliced grilled chicken on the lettuce.
- Sprinkle croutons, grated Parmesan cheese, and halved cherry tomatoes over the chicken.

Wrap and Serve:
- Fold in the sides of the tortilla and roll it up tightly, creating a wrap. Slice in half diagonally if desired.
- Serve the Chicken Caesar Salad Wraps immediately, and enjoy!

These wraps make a delicious and satisfying lunch or dinner option, combining the flavors of a classic Caesar salad with the added protein of grilled chicken.

White Chicken Chili

Ingredients:

- 1 lb boneless, skinless chicken breasts, cooked and shredded
- 2 tablespoons olive oil
- 1 large onion, finely chopped
- 3 cloves garlic, minced
- 2 cans (15 oz each) white beans (such as cannellini or great northern), drained and rinsed
- 1 can (4 oz) diced green chilies
- 1 teaspoon ground cumin
- 1 teaspoon ground coriander
- 1/2 teaspoon dried oregano
- 1/2 teaspoon ground chili powder (adjust to taste)
- 4 cups chicken broth
- Salt and black pepper to taste
- 1 cup frozen corn kernels
- 1/2 cup heavy cream (optional)
- Fresh cilantro, chopped (for garnish)
- Shredded Monterey Jack or white cheddar cheese (for garnish)
- Lime wedges (for serving)

Instructions:

Cook and Shred Chicken:
- Cook the chicken breasts by boiling, baking, or using a rotisserie chicken. Shred the cooked chicken using two forks and set aside.

Sauté Onions and Garlic:
- In a large pot, heat olive oil over medium heat. Add chopped onions and sauté until translucent. Add minced garlic and cook for an additional minute until fragrant.

Add Spices:
- Stir in ground cumin, ground coriander, dried oregano, and ground chili powder. Cook for a couple of minutes to toast the spices.

Combine Chicken and Beans:
- Add the shredded chicken, white beans, diced green chilies, and chicken broth to the pot. Season with salt and black pepper. Bring the mixture to a simmer.

Simmer and Add Corn:
- Let the chili simmer for about 15-20 minutes, allowing the flavors to meld. Add frozen corn kernels and continue simmering for an additional 5-7 minutes.

Add Heavy Cream (Optional):
- If desired, add heavy cream to the chili for a creamy texture. Stir well and let it simmer for a few more minutes.

Adjust Seasoning:
- Taste and adjust the seasoning as needed. If you prefer more heat, you can add additional chili powder.

Serve:
- Ladle the White Chicken Chili into bowls. Garnish with chopped fresh cilantro and shredded cheese. Serve with lime wedges on the side.

Enjoy your hearty and flavorful White Chicken Chili, perfect for a cozy dinner or a comforting meal on a chilly day!

Chicken and Vegetable Curry

Ingredients:

- 1.5 lbs boneless, skinless chicken thighs, cut into bite-sized pieces
- 2 tablespoons vegetable oil
- 1 large onion, finely chopped
- 3 cloves garlic, minced
- 1 tablespoon ginger, grated
- 2 tablespoons curry powder
- 1 teaspoon ground turmeric
- 1 teaspoon ground cumin
- 1 teaspoon ground coriander
- 1 teaspoon chili powder (adjust to taste)
- 1 can (14 oz) diced tomatoes
- 1 cup chicken broth
- 1 cup coconut milk
- 2 large potatoes, peeled and diced
- 2 carrots, peeled and sliced
- 1 bell pepper, diced
- 1 cup green beans, trimmed and cut into 1-inch pieces
- Salt and black pepper to taste
- Fresh cilantro, chopped (for garnish)
- Cooked rice or naan bread (for serving)

Instructions:

Sauté Chicken:
- In a large pot or Dutch oven, heat vegetable oil over medium-high heat. Add the chopped chicken pieces and brown them on all sides. Once browned, remove the chicken from the pot and set aside.

Sauté Aromatics:
- In the same pot, add a bit more oil if needed. Sauté the chopped onion until it becomes translucent. Add minced garlic and grated ginger, and sauté for an additional minute until fragrant.

Add Spices:

- Stir in the curry powder, ground turmeric, ground cumin, ground coriander, and chili powder. Cook the spices for a couple of minutes to release their flavors.

Combine Tomatoes and Broth:
- Pour in the diced tomatoes with their juice and chicken broth. Stir well, scraping the bottom of the pot to release any flavorful bits.

Add Chicken Back In:
- Return the browned chicken to the pot, ensuring it's coated in the spice mixture.

Simmer:
- Add coconut milk, diced potatoes, sliced carrots, diced bell pepper, and cut green beans to the pot. Bring the mixture to a simmer.

Cook Until Vegetables are Tender:
- Cover the pot and simmer for about 20-25 minutes, or until the chicken is cooked through, and the vegetables are tender.

Season and Garnish:
- Season the curry with salt and black pepper to taste. Garnish with chopped fresh cilantro.

Serve:
- Serve the Chicken and Vegetable Curry over cooked rice or with naan bread.

Enjoy your homemade Chicken and Vegetable Curry, a comforting and aromatic dish with a perfect blend of spices!

Chicken Stuffed Bell Peppers

Ingredients:

- 4 large bell peppers, halved and seeds removed
- 1 lb ground chicken
- 1 tablespoon olive oil
- 1 onion, finely chopped
- 2 cloves garlic, minced
- 1 cup cooked quinoa or rice
- 1 cup black beans, drained and rinsed
- 1 cup corn kernels (fresh or frozen)
- 1 teaspoon ground cumin
- 1 teaspoon chili powder
- 1/2 teaspoon paprika
- Salt and black pepper to taste
- 1 cup tomato sauce
- 1 cup shredded cheese (cheddar, Monterey Jack, or your choice)
- Fresh cilantro or parsley for garnish

Instructions:

Preheat Oven:
- Preheat your oven to 375°F (190°C).

Prepare Bell Peppers:
- Cut the bell peppers in half lengthwise and remove the seeds and membranes. Place the pepper halves in a baking dish.

Sauté Chicken and Vegetables:
- In a skillet, heat olive oil over medium heat. Add chopped onions and garlic, sauté until softened.
- Add ground chicken to the skillet and cook until browned. Break it apart with a spoon as it cooks.
- Add cooked quinoa or rice, black beans, corn, ground cumin, chili powder, paprika, salt, and black pepper. Mix well and cook for a few more minutes until everything is heated through.

Stuff Bell Peppers:
- Spoon the chicken and vegetable mixture into the halved bell peppers, pressing down gently to pack the filling.

Top with Tomato Sauce and Cheese:

- Pour tomato sauce over the stuffed peppers, ensuring each one is covered. Sprinkle shredded cheese over the top.

Bake:
- Cover the baking dish with aluminum foil and bake in the preheated oven for 25-30 minutes or until the peppers are tender.

Broil (Optional):
- If you want a golden, bubbly top, you can remove the foil and broil for an additional 2-3 minutes, watching carefully to avoid burning.

Garnish and Serve:
- Remove from the oven, garnish with fresh cilantro or parsley, and serve.

These Chicken Stuffed Bell Peppers make for a satisfying and healthy meal. Enjoy!

Honey Balsamic Glazed Chicken Thighs

Ingredients:

- 4-6 bone-in, skin-on chicken thighs
- Salt and black pepper to taste
- 2 tablespoons olive oil
- 1/4 cup balsamic vinegar
- 3 tablespoons honey
- 2 cloves garlic, minced
- 1 teaspoon Dijon mustard
- 1 teaspoon dried thyme (or 1 tablespoon fresh thyme leaves)
- Fresh parsley, chopped (for garnish)

Instructions:

Preheat Oven:
- Preheat your oven to 400°F (200°C).

Season Chicken Thighs:
- Pat the chicken thighs dry with paper towels. Season both sides with salt and black pepper.

Sear Chicken:
- Heat olive oil in an oven-safe skillet over medium-high heat. Add the chicken thighs, skin side down, and sear until golden brown, about 3-4 minutes per side. Transfer the chicken to a plate.

Prepare Glaze:
- In a bowl, whisk together balsamic vinegar, honey, minced garlic, Dijon mustard, and dried thyme.

Glaze Chicken:
- Pour the balsamic glaze over the seared chicken thighs, ensuring they are well-coated.

Bake:
- Transfer the skillet to the preheated oven and bake for 25-30 minutes or until the chicken is cooked through and registers an internal temperature of 165°F (74°C).

Baste:
- Baste the chicken with the glaze halfway through the cooking time.

Garnish and Serve:

- Remove from the oven, garnish with chopped fresh parsley, and serve the Honey Balsamic Glazed Chicken Thighs hot.

This dish pairs well with a variety of sides such as roasted vegetables, mashed potatoes, or a fresh salad. Enjoy your flavorful and glazed chicken thighs!

Chicken Florentine

Ingredients:

- 4 boneless, skinless chicken breasts
- Salt and black pepper to taste
- 2 tablespoons olive oil
- 4 cloves garlic, minced
- 1 cup chicken broth
- 1 cup heavy cream
- 1 cup grated Parmesan cheese
- 1 teaspoon dried Italian herbs (basil, oregano, thyme)
- 4 cups fresh spinach, chopped
- 1/2 cup sun-dried tomatoes, chopped (optional)
- Lemon wedges for serving
- Cooked pasta or rice (optional, for serving)

Instructions:

Season Chicken:
- Season chicken breasts with salt and black pepper.

Sear Chicken:
- In a large skillet, heat olive oil over medium-high heat. Add chicken breasts and sear on both sides until golden brown and cooked through. Remove chicken from the skillet and set aside.

Sauté Garlic:
- In the same skillet, add minced garlic and sauté for about 1 minute until fragrant.

Prepare Sauce:
- Pour in chicken broth, scraping the bottom of the skillet to deglaze. Add heavy cream, grated Parmesan cheese, and dried Italian herbs. Stir well until the cheese is melted and the sauce is smooth.

Add Spinach and Tomatoes:
- Add chopped spinach to the sauce and cook until wilted. If using sun-dried tomatoes, add them to the skillet as well.

Return Chicken to Skillet:
- Return the seared chicken breasts to the skillet, nestling them into the creamy spinach sauce.

Simmer:

- Simmer for an additional 5-7 minutes until the chicken is heated through and the flavors meld.

Adjust Seasoning:
- Taste the sauce and adjust seasoning with salt and pepper if needed.

Serve:
- Serve Chicken Florentine over cooked pasta or rice, if desired. Drizzle the creamy sauce over the chicken, and garnish with lemon wedges.

Enjoy this comforting and flavorful Chicken Florentine for a delicious meal!

Szechuan Chicken

Ingredients:

For the Marinade:

- 1 lb boneless, skinless chicken breasts, cut into bite-sized pieces
- 2 tablespoons soy sauce
- 1 tablespoon rice vinegar
- 1 tablespoon cornstarch

For the Sauce:

- 3 tablespoons soy sauce
- 2 tablespoons hoisin sauce
- 2 tablespoons rice vinegar
- 1 tablespoon dark soy sauce
- 1 tablespoon sugar
- 1 teaspoon cornstarch

For the Stir-Fry:

- 2 tablespoons vegetable oil
- 3 cloves garlic, minced
- 1 tablespoon fresh ginger, grated
- 1-2 teaspoons Szechuan peppercorns (adjust to taste)
- 1 teaspoon red pepper flakes (adjust to taste)
- 1 bell pepper, thinly sliced
- 1 cup snow peas, trimmed
- 4-5 green onions, sliced
- Cooked white rice for serving

Instructions:

Marinate Chicken:
- In a bowl, combine the marinade ingredients: soy sauce, rice vinegar, and cornstarch. Add the chicken pieces, ensuring they are well-coated. Let it marinate for at least 15-20 minutes.

Prepare Sauce:

- In another bowl, whisk together the sauce ingredients: soy sauce, hoisin sauce, rice vinegar, dark soy sauce, sugar, and cornstarch. Set aside.

Stir-Fry:
- Heat vegetable oil in a wok or large skillet over high heat. Add garlic, ginger, Szechuan peppercorns, and red pepper flakes. Stir-fry for about 30 seconds until fragrant.

Cook Chicken:
- Add the marinated chicken to the wok and stir-fry until the chicken is cooked through and golden brown.

Add Vegetables:
- Add sliced bell pepper and snow peas to the wok. Stir-fry for an additional 2-3 minutes until the vegetables are crisp-tender.

Add Sauce:
- Pour the prepared sauce over the chicken and vegetables. Stir well to coat everything evenly.

Finish and Serve:
- Add sliced green onions and continue to stir-fry for another minute until the sauce thickens and coats the ingredients.

Serve:
- Serve the Szechuan Chicken over cooked white rice.

Adjust the level of spiciness to your liking by increasing or decreasing the amount of Szechuan peppercorns and red pepper flakes. Enjoy the fiery and flavorful Szechuan Chicken!

Chicken Quesadillas

Ingredients:

- 2 cups cooked and shredded chicken (rotisserie chicken works well)
- 1 cup shredded cheddar cheese
- 1 cup shredded Monterey Jack cheese
- 1/2 cup diced bell peppers (any color)
- 1/2 cup diced onions
- 1/4 cup chopped fresh cilantro
- 1 teaspoon ground cumin
- 1 teaspoon chili powder
- Salt and black pepper to taste
- 4 large flour tortillas
- 2 tablespoons vegetable oil
- Salsa, guacamole, and sour cream for serving

Instructions:

Prepare Chicken Mixture:
- In a bowl, combine the shredded chicken, cheddar cheese, Monterey Jack cheese, diced bell peppers, diced onions, chopped cilantro, ground cumin, chili powder, salt, and black pepper. Mix well.

Assemble Quesadillas:
- Lay out the tortillas and divide the chicken mixture evenly on one half of each tortilla. Fold the other half over to create a semi-circle.

Cook Quesadillas:
- Heat a large skillet or griddle over medium heat. Brush one side of each quesadilla with vegetable oil.
- Place the quesadillas, oiled side down, onto the skillet. Cook for 2-3 minutes until the bottom is golden brown.

Flip and Cook:
- Carefully flip the quesadillas and cook the other side until it's golden brown and the cheese is melted.

Serve:
- Remove from the skillet and let them cool for a minute. Cut each quesadilla into wedges and serve with salsa, guacamole, and sour cream on the side.

Enjoy these Chicken Quesadillas as a tasty and satisfying meal!

Chicken Coconut Curry Soup

Ingredients:

- 1 lb boneless, skinless chicken thighs, cut into bite-sized pieces
- Salt and black pepper to taste
- 2 tablespoons vegetable oil
- 1 onion, finely chopped
- 3 cloves garlic, minced
- 1 tablespoon fresh ginger, grated
- 2 tablespoons red curry paste
- 1 can (14 oz) coconut milk
- 4 cups chicken broth
- 2 tablespoons soy sauce
- 1 tablespoon fish sauce
- 1 tablespoon brown sugar
- 1 red bell pepper, thinly sliced
- 1 carrot, julienned
- 1 zucchini, sliced
- 1 cup sliced mushrooms
- 1 cup baby spinach or kale
- Juice of 1 lime
- Fresh cilantro, chopped (for garnish)
- Cooked rice or rice noodles (optional, for serving)

Instructions:

Season and Sear Chicken:
- Season the chicken pieces with salt and black pepper. In a large pot or Dutch oven, heat vegetable oil over medium-high heat. Sear the chicken until browned on all sides. Remove and set aside.

Sauté Aromatics:
- In the same pot, add chopped onion, minced garlic, and grated ginger. Sauté until the onions are softened.

Add Curry Paste:
- Stir in the red curry paste and cook for 1-2 minutes to release its flavors.

Combine Coconut Milk and Broth:
- Pour in coconut milk, chicken broth, soy sauce, fish sauce, and brown sugar. Stir well to combine.

Simmer:
- Add the seared chicken back to the pot. Bring the soup to a simmer and let it cook for 10-15 minutes to allow the flavors to meld.

Add Vegetables:
- Add sliced red bell pepper, julienned carrot, zucchini slices, and mushrooms. Simmer for an additional 5-7 minutes until the vegetables are tender.

Finish Soup:
- Stir in baby spinach or kale until wilted. Add lime juice and adjust the seasoning if needed.

Serve:
- Ladle the Chicken Coconut Curry Soup into bowls. If desired, serve over cooked rice or rice noodles. Garnish with chopped cilantro.

Enjoy the comforting warmth and aromatic flavors of this Chicken Coconut Curry Soup!

Cajun Chicken and Rice

Ingredients:

- 1.5 lbs boneless, skinless chicken thighs, cut into bite-sized pieces
- 2 tablespoons Cajun seasoning
- Salt and black pepper to taste
- 2 tablespoons olive oil
- 1 onion, finely chopped
- 1 bell pepper, diced
- 3 celery stalks, diced
- 3 cloves garlic, minced
- 1 cup long-grain white rice
- 1 can (14 oz) diced tomatoes, undrained
- 1 cup chicken broth
- 1 teaspoon dried thyme
- 1 teaspoon dried oregano
- 1/2 teaspoon cayenne pepper (adjust to taste)
- 1 bay leaf
- Green onions, chopped (for garnish)
- Fresh parsley, chopped (for garnish)

Instructions:

Season Chicken:
- In a bowl, season the chicken pieces with Cajun seasoning, salt, and black pepper. Toss to coat evenly.

Sear Chicken:
- Heat olive oil in a large, deep skillet or Dutch oven over medium-high heat. Add the seasoned chicken and sear until browned on all sides. Remove the chicken from the skillet and set aside.

Sauté Vegetables:
- In the same skillet, add chopped onion, diced bell pepper, diced celery, and minced garlic. Sauté until the vegetables are softened.

Add Rice:
- Stir in the white rice and cook for a couple of minutes until the rice is lightly toasted.

Combine Ingredients:

- Return the seared chicken to the skillet. Add diced tomatoes (with their juice), chicken broth, dried thyme, dried oregano, cayenne pepper, and the bay leaf. Stir to combine.

Simmer:
- Bring the mixture to a simmer. Reduce the heat to low, cover the skillet, and let it simmer for 20-25 minutes or until the rice is cooked and the chicken is tender.

Adjust Seasoning:
- Taste and adjust the seasoning with salt, black pepper, or more Cajun seasoning if desired.

Garnish and Serve:
- Remove the bay leaf. Garnish the Cajun Chicken and Rice with chopped green onions and fresh parsley before serving.

Enjoy this flavorful Cajun Chicken and Rice dish as a comforting and satisfying meal!

Mango Habanero Grilled Chicken

Ingredients:

- 4 boneless, skinless chicken breasts
- Salt and black pepper to taste
- 1 cup mango puree (fresh or canned)
- 2 habanero peppers, seeds removed and finely chopped
- 3 tablespoons honey
- 2 tablespoons soy sauce
- 2 tablespoons lime juice
- 2 cloves garlic, minced
- 1 teaspoon grated ginger
- 2 tablespoons vegetable oil (for grilling)
- Fresh cilantro, chopped (for garnish)

Instructions:

Prepare Marinade:
- In a bowl, whisk together mango puree, finely chopped habanero peppers, honey, soy sauce, lime juice, minced garlic, and grated ginger. Season with salt and black pepper to taste.

Marinate Chicken:
- Place the chicken breasts in a resealable plastic bag or shallow dish. Pour half of the mango habanero marinade over the chicken, ensuring it's well-coated. Reserve the other half for basting and serving. Seal the bag or cover the dish and refrigerate for at least 30 minutes to marinate. For more flavor, you can marinate for a few hours or overnight.

Preheat Grill:
- Preheat your grill to medium-high heat.

Grill Chicken:
- Remove the chicken from the marinade and discard the used marinade. Brush the grill grates with vegetable oil to prevent sticking. Place the chicken on the preheated grill and cook for about 6-8 minutes per side, or until the internal temperature reaches 165°F (74°C) and the chicken is cooked through. Baste the chicken with the reserved marinade during grilling.

Rest and Garnish:

- Remove the chicken from the grill and let it rest for a few minutes before serving.

Serve:
- Drizzle the grilled Mango Habanero Chicken with any remaining marinade and garnish with chopped fresh cilantro. Serve hot.

Enjoy the sweet and spicy kick of Mango Habanero Grilled Chicken! It pairs well with rice, grilled vegetables, or a refreshing salad.

www.ingramcontent.com/pod-product-compliance
Lightning Source LLC
LaVergne TN
LVHW061939070526
838199LV00060B/3874